LONDON HAS A GARDEN

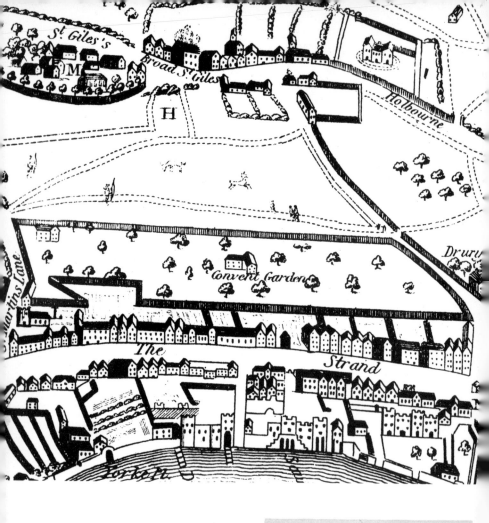

Shakespearean

Clemence Dane

LONDON
HAS A GARDEN

London

MICHAEL JOSEPH

First published by
MICHAEL JOSEPH LTD
26 Bloomsbury Street
London, W.C.1
1964

Set and printed in Great Britain by Unwin Brothers Limited
at the Gresham Press, Woking, in Walbaum type, twelve point,
leaded, and bound by James Burn at Esher, Surrey

In memory of
MICHAEL JOSEPH

It is a frail memory that
remembers but present things

Ben Jonson

CHAPTERS

The author would like to thank
Suhrkamp Verlag, Frankfurt, and
Methuen & Co. Ltd. for permission
to quote from *Die Dreigroschenoper*
by Bertholt Brecht

I

Introduces the Garden

The biggest personality I have ever met was not a person but a place, a plot of land bounded by a Lane, a Long Acre, a Churchyard and a Strand. It was once the garden and grave-yard of a 'covent' of monks: London used to be full of such covents—convents—both for men and women. The square has been known as Frère Pye's Garden, the Covent Garden, Coven Garden, the Common Garden or Covent Garden Market. But most Londoners call it, short and sweet, 'The Garden'.

The word is a sort of caress; for English townspeople are rural at remove, with 'a little place in the country' as the private dream of hard work rewarded in old age. What is London itself but a tiny walled-in Roman city surrounded by an ever enlarging network of snared villages? Wherever there is a railed-in triangular patch of grass with a pub at the corner, there, in spite of ribbon-building and super-markets, was once a village green. Today, overwhelmed by traffic, speculators, factories, dormitories and taxation, city-swallowed villagers and country-townsmen still cling to their token gardens.

The gardens come all shapes and sizes. Geraniums are bedded out in oblongs edged with privet, pink hawthorn and laburnum clash like cymbals against Victorian red brick, and the rockeries hang like patchwork-quilts where-ever the little houses stand high above the by-passers and the passers-by. Roadside planting, nationalized, has become a minor art, and the average householder, usually his own gardener and lawn-mower, responds to the new challenge. The Cockney's instinct for self-preservation is also behind

9

it. Lord Taylor of Harlow, recently addressing the Royal
Society of Health, told the members that thirty per cent of
the population of England suffered from 'a sub-clinical
neurosis syndrome'. The cure he urged was plenty of work,
not so much glass in modern buildings, and—a garden.
'The need for a garden was greater today than ever before.
In its cultivation people could find peace of mind.'

'Huh! I always knew it,' says the Londoner. Indeed
since Norman times London has been a city of gardens.
When Boadicea declared war on the Romans 'the sweetness
of the place' tempted some to stay behind, to their own
destruction. There was a vineyard near the Tower in King
Stephen's time, and a writer in the next reign says that
'adjoining the houses on all sides lie the gardens of those
citizens that dwell in the suburbs, which are well-furnished
with trees, spacious and beautiful.' Henry III writes to an
underling telling him to buy 'certain perie plants'—pear-
trees—'to set the same in my place without the Tower of
London.'

Like master like man. Stow tells us that on the eve of
St John the Baptist every man's door was shadowed with
green birch, long fennel, St John's wort, orpin, white
lilies and such-like, garnished with garlands of beautiful
flowers. I think by 'beautiful' he means cultivated; for
in those days wild-flowers were everywhere. As late as 1633
the small wild bugloss grew upon the dry ditch banks of
Piccadilly.

So when Shakespeare makes Richard III say to an attend-
ant bishop:

> 'My lord of Ely . . . when I was last in Holborn
> I saw good strawberries in your garden there.
> I do beseech you send for some of them,'

he isn't brilliantly inventing for the sake of sounding
natural. We have the conversation itself. ' "My Lord,"
(said the Duke of Gloucester, afterwards Richard III),

"you have very good strawberries at your garden in Holborn; I require you let us have a mess of them." "Gladly, my lord,' quoth he (the Bishop of Ely), "would God I had some better thing as ready to your pleasure as that,"—and therewithal, in haste, he sent his servant for a mess of strawberries.'

The request bears out the stories of Richard's tact. Back-yard or bishop's palace, who isn't proud of his garden's first strawberries—or his roses? When Queen Elizabeth arranged for a later Bishop of Ely to lease the gatehouse of his palace to her Captain of the Guard the ground-rent was a red rose, and the Bishop charged his tenant ten loads of hay and ten pounds a year, with the right to walk in the garden and to pick yearly *twenty bushels of roses*.

The Londoner continued to sit under his own vine and fig-tree for centuries. There is a fig-tree by the river just opposite Cleopatra's Needle which in the forties still bore figs. In the autumns of the war years when I took my terrier for his inevitable after-the-All-Clear run I used to pick up the windfalls and bring them home—they made an excellent pickle. As for vines, wine was still made in the nineteenth century from a vine growing in St Martin's Lane. The London wines, it is said, were mainly red, like a good Burgundy, and there were several notable vineyards, which seems impossible till one remembers how small London was, not so long ago. There were 'much over a hundred thousand inhabitants' at the beginning of the eighteenth century, which, the writer implies, was a huge population. It explains to us why London was for so long a city of gardens. Greater London did not exist. People hired escorts or waited to travel in a crowd before risking a journey to Kensington. Mrs Siddons settled down in a country cottage on Paddington Green. A friend of mine— he died when I was well over thirty—once told me that he lived as a boy in the last house in London. It lay east of Marble Arch. As late as 1866 *The Cornhill* printed an account of a gardener, still alive, who remembered the days

11

when there were 'thirteen thousand acres of vegetables and fruit-trees within four miles of Charing Cross'. This was before the Kensington nurseries were levelled and 'sown with International Exhibition temples,' as the indignant writer put it. He clearly feels about those fore-runners of the Natural History Museum and the Albert Hall as we feel about the skyscrapers in Knightsbridge and the single monster which overlooks the gardens of Buckingham Palace.

On the credit side, the twentieth century's display of flowers in the London parks grows more brilliant every year. The laurels in the squares, once as dusty as ill-kept bronzes, are being replaced by forsythias, prunus and buddleia. Cement flower-tubs dumped in odd corners are filled and watered. There is a bed of heart's-ease on the Albert Bridge roundabout, wallflowers at the top of Launceston Place, and a street of young cherry-trees off the King's Road. Rhododendrons flourish in Parliament Square, and a terrace of flowering shrubs lies north of Nelson's Column where the Tree, Norway's yearly Christmas present, is set up each December.

But in London's own special Garden there is no green to rest the eye; for the trees and flowering lawns of the churchyard are tucked away behind the market church. In the eternal war between grass and brick, brick has won a hateful victory over the fields that used to run from the tiny Roman city clear down to the marshes of Westminster. There was always a fringe of houses and gardens running along the south side of the Strand; but until the reign of the first Elizabeth the most westerly establishment of importance on the north side was Drury House, from which Drury Lane got its name.

Then, early in Queen Elizabeth's time, Sir William Cecil, later the Lord of Burleigh, established himself between the Lane and the present Burleigh Street. He was the best businessman in England: it was inevitable that he should foresee how valuable the north side of the Strand was

12

going to be. Stow says that the great prime minister took over a house 'begun in the reign of Edward VI of brick and timber, very large and spacious,' and a London citizen records that the Queen went to inspect the place before it was even finished.

'The same night the Queen's grace went by Clerkenwell over the fields unto the Savoy unto master secretary Cecil to supper . . . and there was great cheer till midnight.'

That was in 1563. She visited him again when the anger against Spain was at its height. Going through a low doorway she was desired to stoop her head, and returned: 'I will stoop for your master; but not for the King of Spain.' And again when Burleigh was old and sick she came to see him and coaxed him to eat, herself taking a spoon and feeding him. That was a good friendship between a great man and a great woman.

Burleigh leased part of his orchard from his neighbours, the Russells, who in Henry VIII's time had acquired the whole northern stretch of the Strand and the open country behind it, including Covent Garden and the Long Acre. Under Edward VI the head of the Russells became Earl of Bedford. The fifth Earl got leave from Charles I to build on the Covent Garden site north of the wall-terrace of his own garden. He called in Inigo Jones, and within five years the general scheme had been realized. Instead of fields there was to be a square with broad streets, a church and a Piazza running north and east.

The new square was so sensationally magnificent that Brome, Ben Jonson's protégé and a writer of amusing topical pieces, opens one of his comedies, 'Covent Garden Weeded', with 'a great builder' showing a V.I.P. the new square. The magistrate, a Puritan, admires everything, but is anxious that only the right people should be allowed as tenants.

THE V.I.P.: Marry sir! This is something like! Here's architecture

13

expressed indeed! It is a most sightly situation, and fit for gentry and nobility.

THE BUILDER: When it is all finished, doubtless it will be handsome.

THE V.I.P.: It will be glorious: and yond magnificent piece, the Piazzo, will excel that at Venice, by hearsay, (I ne'er travell'd). A hearty blessing on their brains, honours and wealths, that are projectors, furtherers and performers of such great works. . . . I like your row of houses most uncomparably.

THE BUILDER: I have pil'd up a leash of a thousand pounds in walls and windows there.

THE V.I.P.: It will come again with large increase. You cannot think how I am taken with that row. How even and straight they are. . . . The surveyor (what e'er he was) has manifested himself the master of his great art. How he has wedded strength to beauty; state to uniformity; commodiousness with perspicuity! All, all as't should be!

Unfortunately the 'Piazzo' was never completed. The Duke had paid a heavy fine for breaking the building regulations—we should call it an improvement tax—and his economical heirs used this as an excuse to ruin Inigo's splendid design. The terraced wall of Bedford House, they argued, would serve well enough to complete the south side of the square.

Bedford House was pulled down centuries ago; but I have a dim recollection of being shown, long before the last war, a portion of the ancient garden-wall, built into a house off Maiden Lane.

In the shadow of this terrace-wall at the end of the Bedford House garden smallholders were allowed to sell fruit, vegetables and flowers. Their open stands soon became covered booths and the Square a popular marketing-place; though the seats for shoppers under a pleasant grotto of elms came later.

This phase of the Garden's social life ended with the Civil War and the execution of the King in 1649; but the church was approved by the new authorities, which suggests

that the curate of St Paul's must have been either very
discreet or very much a Cromwellian; for public worship
had become a risky business for members of the established
church. Evelyn tells us that as late as 1657—only three
years before the Restoration—he was attending a Communion Service, not in St Paul's, Covent Garden, but in
Burleigh's chapel in the great house at the east end of the
Garden. It was Christmas morning. Suddenly a horde of
Puritan soldiers broke in and rounded up the entire congregation.

'These wretched miscreants held their muskets against us as
we came up to receive the Sacred Elements, as if they would
have shot us at the Altar.'

Evelyn himself was detained for several days in Burleigh
House and then was faced by Macarthy-type inquisitors.

'They took my name and abode,' (the phrase has changed by
one word only in three hundred years!) 'and examined me
why, contrary to an ordinance made that none should any
longer observe the superstitious time of the Nativity, (so
esteemed by them) I durst offend . . . and particularly pray for
Charles Stuart, for which we had no Scripture . . . with other
frivolous and insnaring questions, with much threatening, and
finding no colour to detain me longer, with much pity of my
ignorance, they dismiss'd me.'

One can be sure that no pagan holly nor Druidical
mistletoe was sold in the Garden that Christmas.

But Cromwell died the following year, leaving England
very ready for a change of rulers. Evelyn makes that plain
in his account of Cromwell's funeral. Cromwell lay in state
in Somerset House, the palace of the Queen he had wid-
owed. Evelyn had relatives living in Covent Garden, and
would have seen the rowdy procession.

'It was the joyfullest funeral I ever saw, for there were none
that cried but dogs, which the soldiers hooted away with a barbarous noise, drinking and taking tobacco as they went.'

15

When the dead King's son came back the nation behaved like a family who had not had a holiday for twenty years. Charles II arrived on his birthday, riding through ways strawed with flowers, the bells ringing, the streets hung with tapestry, fountains running with wine. The King was seven hours passing through the City 'even from two in the afternoon till nine at night. I stood in the Strand,' says Evelyn, 'and beheld it and blessed God . . . for such a Restoration was never seen in the mention of any history . . . nor so joyful a day and so bright ever seen in this nation.'

After that reception it was inevitable that Charles should be labelled for all time 'the Merry Monarch', if only because he had made everyone remember that Puritania had once been called 'Merry England'. Yet 'merry' is an odd label for the cynical, tolerant masquerader whom nobody could intimidate and nobody surprise. It no more describes Charles himself than the word 'Stuart' gives us his quality.

Romantic novelists and playwrights have made the Stuarts into romantic creatures, history's film-stars; but though they were endowed with all the traditional christening gifts, the charm that is better than beauty, great expectations and the rest, the bad fairy always turned up at the last moment and added the one gift which ruined the luck—the gift for doing the right thing at the wrong moment. If only Prince Charles had not turned back at Derby—if only Mary Stuart's white hand had not betrayed her in the boat—if only James II had not run away! If—if—!

Charles II is the single and singular exception. His charm and his power of creating affection are the proper fairy-tale Stuart qualities; but he was not obstinate, he had more brains in his little finger than all his Stuart ancestors put together and he knew how to wait for the right moment. His paternal grandfather was James of Scotland, the wisest fool in Christendom; but his other grandfather

16

was Henry of Navarre, the king who restored France and devised that Magna Carta of religious freedom, the Edict of Nantes.

The resemblance between Henry the Great of France and his English grandson is startling. The Navarrese knew all about poverty, exile and petty humiliations. Even when he had beaten his enemies he still had to change his religion in order to become king of France. He said: 'Paris is worth a mass,' and changed it.

As the grandfather, so the grandson. When King Charles was restored he showed no rancour, but behaved as if England were a woman distracted by a mental illness— the Civil War—and his job was to coax her back to normal life. He made her laugh. He made love to her. Sometimes he gave her shock treatment. She had worn tightly laced Puritan corsets for thirty years. He cut the strings. She wanted the English Court to outshine the Court of France, where the great Henry's other grandson reigned, a central sun. Charles had neither the cash nor the inclination to create a Versailles or a Louvre, but he made the English Court a lively place; though he had far too much sense and humour to imitate Louis the Fourteenth's pomposities.

Both cousins inherited their grandfather's way with women; but, as Pepys noted, when the King of France visited his mistresses 'he went publicly and his trumpets and kettledrums with him'; while the King of England, on at least one occasion, preferred climbing over the wall. But he was quite open about his love-affairs, and the nation, like Pepys, found the ladies fascinating but the publicity upsetting.

His critics were loud also against his extravagance, his informality and the politic delaying tactics which they took for laziness. Yet King Charles continued to win the last round in every struggle. He left behind him a calmed, civilized and prosperous England, and was mourned as few kings are mourned.

How did he manage it? Dryden, who knew him well, suggests that his early misfortunes afforded him an opportunity which is rarely allowed to sovereign princes, 'I mean of travelling and being conversant in the most polished Courts of Europe, and thereby of cultivating a spirit which was formed by nature to receive the impressions of a generous and gallant education.'

It is a reasonable explanation, but it is not a complete one. The King's brother, the future James II, had been afforded the same opportunities and had later done excellent service as a chief of the Navy, and yet the country hated him long before he became king and gave it just cause to hate him.

Perhaps the wax effigy at Westminster gives us a clue. It is startlingly unlike the heavy representations of him in paint and stone made by his own artists. The mask does not belong to its period at all. It is more like the head of a lively, youngish man of the middle twentieth century. Its expression of humour, disillusionment and tolerance is one that we, with two world wars behind us, recognize and can interpret only too easily. 'He has been through the war and he has been through the peace. He has settled for it; but he is bone-tired.'

It is difficult to believe that his own factious age at all understood that expression; but it is one which must have given him a special influence over his subjects. To be a king and yet so easy a human-being, to be able to put off royalty and yet at the end of a long reign to be so completely established in rule, that would impress, that would fascinate. As for his Black Boy features—it is true that Charles called himself an 'ugly fellow', but I doubt if we should agree with him. We should be much more likely to think him handsome, or at any rate to recognize in his ugliness a something uninvented in his lifetime—'star quality'.

Many endearing tales are told of him. One of the best is Steele's account of how King Charles dines in the City with the Lord Mayor, Sir Robert Viner.

18

'Sir Robert was a very loyal man . . . but what with the joy
he felt at heart for the honour done him by his Prince, and thro'
the warmth he was in with continual toasting healths to the
Royal Family, his Lordship grew a little fond of his Majesty, and
entered into a familiarity not altogether so graceful in so public
a place. The King understood very well how to extricate himself
on all kinds of difficulties, and with an hint to the company to
avoid ceremony, stole off and made towards his coach, which
stood ready for him in the Guildhall Yard: But the Mayor liked
his company so well, and was grown so intimate, that he pursued
him hastily, and catching him fast by the hand, cried out with
a vehement oath and accent, "Sir, you shall stay and take t'other
bottle." The airy monarch looked kindly at him over his shoulder,
and with a smile and graceful air, (for I saw him at the time, and
do now) repeated this line of the old song:
 ' "He that's drunk is as great as a King."
and immediately returned back and complied with his landlord.
I saw the passage; and I assure you it's very true.'

Halifax said that the King's greatest fault was his love
of sauntering—mental sauntering, for he could out-walk
anyone. But King Charles sauntered his way through
difficulties which had destroyed his conscientious father and
were to wreck his obstinate brother. It is pleasant to
remember that he knew and used the Garden byways,
sauntering up Bow Street to call on his friend William
Wycherley when the dramatist was ill of a fever.

Bow Street in those days ended in a blockade of houses
and gardens, and beyond lay the open fields. Pepys gives
us a vivid sketch of the extraordinary mixture of Inigo
Jones elegance with Bo-Peep charm.

'1st May, 1667. To Westminster: in the way meeting many
milk-maids with their garlands upon their pails, dancing with a
fiddler before them; and saw pretty Nelly standing at her
lodgings door in Drury Lane in her smock sleeves and bodice,
looking upon one: she seemed a mighty pretty creature.'

Nell Gwynne has gone on seeming a mighty pretty
creature to the English from that day to this. They did not

love her because she was a fine comedienne and wit: they loved her because, as Mrs Aphra Behn told her to her face, she had 'an eternal sweetness, youth and air . . . as if you were made on purpose to put the whole world into good humour,' and because she remembered her beginnings and the troubles of poor folk. There is a tradition that she persuaded the King to found the Chelsea Royal Hospital for invalid soldiers, and I found out by chance a year or two ago that the hospital has not forgotten her.

There is a dignified old Chelsea pensioner who comes to the L.C.C. pottery-classes in Bolt Court. He is proud of the hospital, and he has a charming devotion to the memory of Nell Gywnne. He came at first in his seventeenth-century uniform to sit as a model for the painting-class next door to the clay-room, and in going in and out he used to linger to watch wheels revolving and coil-pots taking shape, so fascinated that at last we persuaded him to try his hand. He could not see very well and had nothing but a tiny print and an enlarging-glass to guide him; but his finger-tips had eyes, and he ended by modelling a portrait-bust of Nell Gwynne that looked like a Della Robbia. The head was exhibited, and he was offered a large sum of money for it. But no, he had made it for Nell Gwynne's Hospital, and to the Hospital he gave it. It stands today outside the Governor's office-door smiling.

It was something to be loved by a King of England and to be remembered with affection as he lay dying—'Let not poor Nelly starve!'—but to be loved after three hundred years as my old friend loved Nell Gwynne's memory does not happen to many women. Ellen Terry is the only other actress I can think of who has left behind her so strong an impression of laughter, charm and wildness—a scent of sweet-briar in the air. And she, too, belonged to Covent Garden. The Lyceum stage-door is in Burleigh Street.

Nell Gwynne's Drury Lane soon changed character. The aristocrats of the Garden needed increasing supplies of fruit and vegetables, and within a few years a licensed market was held on Tuesdays, Thursdays and Fridays, 'well served with choice goods,' which means, I suppose, that there was beginning to be a demand for exotics as well as the usual English fruits and summer flowers. The age was interested in horticulture. Bacon had loved to have flowers on his table, and his gardens and walks at Gorhambury were 'delicious'—Aubrey's word. Aubrey also says that Charles I was another garden lover. Philip, the younger brother of the Pembroke who may have been Shakespeare's Mr W.H., was a close friend of the King's. 'King Charles Ist did love Wilton above all places. . . . It was He that did put Philip (Ist) Earl of Pembroke upon making this magnificent garden . . . the third garden of the Italian mode. But in the time of king Charles IId gardening was much improved and became common: I do believe, I may modestly affirm, that there is now [1691] ten times as much gardening about London as there was in 1660; and we have been since that time much improved in foreign plants, especially since about 1683, there have been exotic plants brought into England, no less than seven thousand.'

Parkinson had published his *Paradisus*, Evelyn his *Sylva*, and John Ray, 'the greatest o' them all' according to Kipling, had written a general history of plants in unfamiliar Latin as well as a book of proverbs in familiar English. 'Anything for a quiet life!'—'That was laid on with a trowel.'—'Live and let live!' We all quote John Ray.

The newly founded Royal Society even gave its blessing to the potato, and I fancy that I have seen somewhere a picture of King Charles himself confronted by the first hothouse-grown English pineapple. The proud grower is displaying the unique fruit, and the King is inspecting it with his usual air of humorous resignation over the odd jobs his profession required him to perform. It is a far cry from that comical moment to the hungry childhood of Charles Dickens. 'When I had no money I took a turn in Covent Garden and stared at the pineapples.'

Dickens's pre-Victorian Covent Garden of the pine-apples was surrounded by a maze of slums not cleared away till the present century. These slums were almost as old as the Square itself; for as soon as the Garden became 'the heart of the town' the inevitable happened. It was a fine thing for the district that theatres, hotels and smart shops were necessary to supply the handsome new houses, that the King's mistress should live in Drury Court, that the church should be crammed on Sundays and the coffee-houses full throughout the week. Strype snobbishly re-joices over 'this Parish . . . so well inhabited by a mixture of nobility, gentry and wealthy tradesmen, here seated since the fire of London, scarce admitting of any poor, not very pestered with mean courts and alleys, likewise its open and large piazza and garden so delightful to walk in.'

He wrote too soon. Inevitably the slums followed, spreading out over waste spaces like mussel-beds spreading out between the rocks of a foreshore. The main streets might be open and large; but in between lay a maze of in-sanitary alleys and ill-lighted lanes, and the community which dwelt in the airless little courts was rotten with poverty and dangerous with want.

A turning called Rose Street runs north from recent Garrick Street to a tiny courtyard, and in it stands a small, compact tavern called 'The Lamb and Flag'. If you notice it at all you merely think how charming these corners of old London can be. But three hundred years ago it was a sinister corner: it was there, in Rose Alley, that the attack on Dryden took place.

Dryden, Charles II's Poet Laureate, the 'glorious John' of four reigns, was a Covent Garden man. He lived in Long Acre. Another Covent Garden man was Lord Rochester, poet and satirist. He lived in Bow Street. The two men admired each other's work and were friends, as far as friendship was possible in those days between a hard-working professional writer and an amateur who was superior in rank and sixteen years younger.

Rochester's father had been the faithful companion of King Charles in the long years of exile, and at seventeen his son had the run of the Court, an outrageous teenager, the leader of pleasure-mongers who had not half his quality. 'Lord Rochester was of a very bad turn of mind as well as debauched,' says Pope, at second-hand. But those who abused him most bitterly forgot how young he was. King Charles remembered. He was always banishing him for some youthful folly and then forgiving him, a little too soon; perhaps because there was in the King himself a spring of defeated youth which still bubbled up at the most unsuitable moments. When Rochester laughed at everyone, including the King, the King laughed with him.

Unfortunately Rochester did not much care about being laughed at in turn. When that happened he made scenes. Pepys himself saw the sequel to one of them and was horrified; for Pepys kept his lapses to himself and his diary.

'Among the rest of the King's company there was that worthy fellow my lord of Rochester, and Tom Killigrew, whose mirth and raillery offended the former so much that he did give Tom Killigrew a box on the ear in the King's presence, which do much give offence to the people here at Court, to see how cheap the King makes himself, and the more that the King hath not only passed by the thing, and pardoned it to Rochester already, but this very morning the King did publicly walk up and down, and Rochester I saw with him as free as ever, to the King's everlasting shame, to have so idle a rogue his companion.'

But Philip sober was always disarmingly contrite for the misdoings of Philip drunk. Rochester later apologized to the son of the man whom he had insulted, and did it 'solemnly'. Also the King, though he smoothed matters over in public as his way was, had his own methods of dealing with offenders. He sent his obstreperous young friend— Rochester was even then only twenty—on 'a little journey to Paris' as the King put it. He certainly gave him a letter of introduction to his sister; but it is on record that Rochester did not enjoy himself, nor can one think that it was intended that he should.

But there were other sides to Rochester. As a poet he was technically ahead of his age, and as a thinker he never ceased to develop. He was an affectionate if unstable husband, and towards the end of his short life he turned away from all his former interests and seems to have undergone one of those sudden strange conversions that William James writes of in his *Varieties of Religious Experience*.

That happened after increasing illness had sent him home to die. Till then he continued to be the wild-cat of the Court, walking by himself. Some of his exploits are comical, even endearing—his masquerade as an astrologer, and his attempt to kidnap the woman whom he loved and did eventually marry. The blackest mark against him has been, until our own times, his alleged connection with the Rose Alley attack on Dryden. This is the story:

Lord Mulgrave, later another Duke of Buckingham, had written a coarse lampoon upon the Court. The principal targets were the second Duke of Buckingham, the King's mistresses and Rochester. Mulgrave was Dryden's patron, and rumour ran that Dryden had helped him to polish his rather bad verses. It was even said, absurdly, that he had written most of them.

The mere possibility was enough in that ferocious age. Dryden, cutting home past the 'Lamb and Flag' one dark December night, was set upon and brutally cudgelled. The bullies escaped and were never caught; but scandal had it that one of three people had instigated the outrage—the Duchess of Portsmouth through her brother-in-law Pembroke—or Buckingham—or Rochester. Rochester was the most flamboyant of the figures concerned, and so the gossip-writers finally settled between them that his was the hidden hand. But Professor Pinto, whose new biography *Enthusiast in Wit* was recently published, thinks that Pembroke was responsible and gives convincing reasons.

Certainly the breach between Dryden and Rochester is

more likely to have been a matter of different codes than a vulgar business of unsigned attack and crude vengeance. Pope once told Spence, and Spence insists that he meant it kindly, that 'Dorset and Rochester should be considered as holiday writers, as gentlemen that diverted themselves now and then with poetry rather than as poets.' Dryden, on the other hand, was forced by the very nature of his work to have a double standard. In his approach to the art of writing he was meticulous; but as a breadwinner he was not far off the professional journalist point of view. His literary sincerity cannot be impeached; but the sincerity of his sentiments is often doubtful, and he saw no harm in giving his public what it wanted.

> 'They who have best succeeded on the stage,
> Have still conform'd their genius to their age. . . .
> Fame then was cheap, and the first comer sped;
> And they have kept it since, by being dead.'

But Rochester had no need to give any public what it wanted. Rochester's bread was secure and his position was secure. His problem was how to weigh-up what his nature truly enjoyed against what it was the fashion to enjoy. He belongs to our own time in his rebellions, his frustrations and his pathological self-knowledge.

> 'Then old age and experience, hand in hand,
> Lead him to death, and make him understand,
> After a search so painful and so long,
> That all his life he has been in the wrong.
> Huddled in dirt the reasoning engine lies,
> Who was so proud, so witty and so wise.'

'That all his life he has been in the wrong.' He can say this of mankind and himself at thirty. It was not the sort of self-revelation possible to Dryden, even at seventy. How should it occur to Dryden to doubt his own judgements or criticise his own achievements? Dryden had the strongest and most flexible mind of any writer of his time. How could Dryden be in the wrong?

Dryden had found himself able, as a professional writer, to mourn Cromwell majestically and welcome Charles II ecstatically all in a year, to uphold the Church of England under a Protestant king and change his religion when a Catholic one succeeded. It is true that when the throne once more changed hands he did not change once more, but submitted to losing the laureateship and was forced (bitterly protesting) to work for his bread till he died—at sixty-nine he bound himself to supply his bookseller with ten thousand verses at sixpence a line.

But he was still the acknowledged ruler of the literary world and its hangers-on, which knew all about his prodigious achievement—the thirty-odd plays, the masques, libretti, satires, poems, operas, discourses, essays, adaptations, prologues and epilogues. He was a giant then and a giant now. In terms of this world and its judgements Dryden obliterates the holiday-writer who was always in the wrong. Then why isn't one wholly sympathetic about that beating-up? Why is Dryden so irritating? I think it must be because he was so invincibly pleased with himself.

The busy author Bayes in Buckingham's play *The Rehearsal* is drawn from more than one original; but Dryden's quality overwhelms the others. *The Rehearsal* is a wildly funny play in its own right, a wicked burlesque of any author directing his own play at any age and in any age. It has the sort of humour that makes you startle other people in a railway-carriage by laughing aloud, and is at its funniest when it hits off Dryden's love of discussing his own methods of work.

BAYES: [*the professional author*] What do you do when you write?
SMITH [*the amateur*]: I take pen, ink and paper and sit down.
BAYES: Now *I* write standing. . . . Another thing is, with what do
    you prepare yourself?
SMITH: Prepare myself? [*aside*] What the devil does the fool
    mean?

BAYES: Why, I'll tell you now what I do. If I am to write familiar things, as sonnets and the like, I make use of stewed prunes only. But when I have a grand design in hand, I ever take physic.

And again—and here the caricaturist is hitting at **Dryden's** reputation for picking other people's brains:

BAYES: I come into a coffee-house or some other place where witty men resort; I make as if I minded nothing; (do you mark?) but as soon as anyone speaks, pop, I slap it down and make that too my own.

But though *The Rehearsal* hits off the failings, it leaves out the genius—and the savagery. Buckingham nags and nips and gets in a nasty bite or two; but when Dryden retaliates it is the elephant slow-turning on the mongrel at his heels.

> 'A man so various that he seem'd to be
> Not one, but all mankind's Epitome.'

Stamp!

> 'Stiff in opinions, always in the wrong;
> Was everything by starts, and nothing long:'

Stamp!

> 'But in the course of one revolving moon
> Was chemist, fiddler, statesman and buffoon.'

Stamp! Stamp! Stamp! *Stamp!*

And yet, believe it or not, Dryden assured everyone that, though the sketch was the best thing he ever did, there was no offence in it, no offence in the world.

"The character . . . is not bloody, but it is ridiculous enough, and he for whom it was intended was too witty to resent it as an injury. If I had railed I might have suffered for it justly, but—" the Bayes touch, "I managed my own work

27

more happily, perhaps because more dexterously. I avoided the mention of great crimes, and applied myself to the representing of blind sides and little extravagancies . . . It succeeded as I wished. The jest went round, and he was laughed at in his turn who began the frolic."

The frolic! He calls the character of Zimri in *Absalom and Achitophel* a frolic! No wonder that the plump man with a down look was stared upon with passionate respect by a schoolboy called Alexander Pope. That crippled child, not yet in his teens, was to write a few years later:

> 'Yes, I am proud. I must be proud to see
> Men not afraid of God afraid of me.'

A king looked upon his heir that day in Will's Coffee House.

'Will's' was only one of several famous conversation centres in the Garden. After Dryden's death 'Button's', just opposite, became the most popular, with Addison as the reigning Jupiter. But though the eighteenth century continued to be the age of the wits, 'the town' was moving westward. When Bedford House was pulled down early in the days of Queen Anne, Tavistock Street was built on the site of the stables, and ran as far as a horse-pond hard by the present Wellington Street. Then it joined York Street, which was built seventy years earlier and named after the Duke of York who became James II.

York Street in its time has housed several gods. The Opium Eater dreamed his dreams there. There is a link with Donne. Elliston, the actor-manager, lived in York Street, and so did Mrs Pritchard, Mrs Siddons's forerunner and only rival.

'She was a vulgar woman, she called a gown a gownd,' said Johnson, who didn't admire Mrs Pritchard; but her Lady Macbeth was long remembered by theatre audiences. Indeed the respect in which it was held later caused the great Mr Sheridan to make a fool of himself.

28

Sheridan was in charge at Drury Lane when Mrs Siddons gave her first London performance in what she called 'the grand, fiendish part', and while she was dressing and already in a state of nerves he came panicking to her dressing-room, though as the son of an actor he ought to have known better. But his spies had reported that Mrs Siddons meant to *put down the candle in the sleep-walking scene*, and that was treason, that was blasphemy: Mrs Pritchard had always held on to it, hand-washing or no hand-washing. The audience would never permit such an innovation. It would rage.

However Mrs Siddons refused to listen to him, and when she put down the candle on that most memorable of all Drury Lane first nights the hypnotized audience raged indeed, but in admiration and delight.

After her day, though Covent Garden and Drury Lane continued to be London's principal theatres, the Garden gradually ceased to be the centre of social life. In the early and middle years of the nineteenth century its main frequenters were journalists, painters, engravers, illustrators, actors, novelists—in short the Dickens crowd. But by the end of the Victorian age there were few of them left; though P. G. Wodehouse writes nostalgically of getting breakfast at The Hummums after a wildish night. The Hummuns was a turkish-bath establishment on the east side of the Market where clients could stay all night, and for many years enormously popular with late-night-finalists.

Physically, too, the square was constantly changing. The Little Piazza lost part of its arcade in 1796. A hundred years later the whole had gone. New streets had been cut through the maze of back-alleys and airless courts. By the time Garrick Street was built the green hedges of St Martin's Lane had given place to a street of houses which ran up to Seven Dials and Cambridge Circus.

East of the Garden the slums lingered till the great thoroughfare, Kingsway, was driven from the Strand at Waterloo Bridge to Holborn, obliterating many historical byways but also giving the district a much-needed spring-cleaning. Barton Barker, writing in 1903, has a weary sigh about it: 'When in some future age of the world the new street from Holborn to the Strand is finished . . . etc.' But in 1905 it was at last opened by King Edward himself, and the catchword of the hour ran: 'Do you know why they pulled down the Aldwych? Because it's in the King's way.'

The local authorities have also been busy in the last fifty years regulating street numbers and eliminating duplicate names, and the Garden has lost Hart Street. Modern maps give five Hart Streets, one between Oxford Street and Carlos Place, another in Bloomsbury, another off Theobald's Road, and two in the City. It is a fair guess that each street was originally the site of a White Hart Inn; for the White Hart, one of the royal badges, has always been a favourite inn name—it is on record that there was a White Hart Inn in the Hart Street off Theobald's Road. There was also one in the Garden itself in Queen Elizabeth's reign, kept by a certain Humphrey Gosling.

'Of virtuous behaviour, a very good archer,
And of honest mirth, a very good company keeper,
So well inclined to poor and rich.
God send more Goslings to be sich.'

And in memory of Gosling and his inn there was a Hart Street in Covent Garden until our own century.

But so many Hart Streets is pretty confusing for the post-man, and the time came when the Post Office began eliminating. Hart Street in Crutched Friars was safe, of course, because of Dick Whittington. After he became Lord Mayor of London he built himself a mansion in Hart Street, and the story goes that he gave a banquet to King Henry V there, the most expensive banquet since Cleopatra melted her pearl in wine; for he threw into the fire sixty thousand pounds worth of the King's I.O.U.s. So nobody could possibly change the name of Whittington's Hart Street.

But the other Hart Streets have no Whittington and no

Gosling to be proud of; it therefore seems unfair that Covent Garden's Hart Street had to become Floral Street while other Hart Streets keep the name.

Then York Street lost its historic label. It became a continuation of Tavistock Street, which pleased nobody. Letters went astray, callers were confused, and it made one look foolish to be always giving one's address as: 'Twelve Tavistock Street, I mean twenty.' Besides, York Street was one of the oldest streets in the Garden; while Tavistock Street at its best had never been more than a modish shopping-centre.

It is surprising that the name survives. When Bedford House was pulled down and the Russell family migrated to Bloomsbury they took the family names with them: there is a Russell Square and a Tavistock Square in Bloomsbury, which is hard on American visitors who want Tavistock Street, Covent Garden, and a gold-mine to taxi-drivers. There was also, facing Tavistock Street, a Tavistock Row; but that vanished with Queen Victoria, and today there is not so much as a plaque to remind the passer-by that Godwin, Shelley's father-in-law, lived there, or that the town once rang with the story of Miss Reay, Lord Sandwich's mistress, who had lodgings in Number 4.

> 'A clergyman, O wicked one,
> In Covent Garden shot her.
> No time to cry upon her God.
> It's hoped He's not forgot her.'

But Number 4 was pulled down long ago, and the site of the Row is now a fenced-in, high-roofed shelter for carts, wooden boxes and the Market cats.

Indeed the Garden today, apart from its theatres, is a business-centre, ranging from garden produce to banks and publishing houses. *Country Life*, appropriately, has settled opposite the Fruit-and-Vegetables, and *The Queen* has offices in Burleigh Street, which is even more appropriate when you remember Elizabeth I's visits to Burleigh. But the Royal Theatres which King Charles set up when he granted patents to Killigrew and Davenant are still the Jachin and Boaz of English theatre.

'And Solomon set up the pillars in the porch of the temple: and he set up the right pillar and called the name thereof Jachin: and he set up the left pillar and called the name thereof Boaz.'

The patents were abolished in the last century; but as you go up Wellington Street from Waterloo Bridge the pillars are still to be seen. The Theatre Royal Drury Lane is only a street away on your right, and, on your left, the Royal Opera House Covent Garden confronts the successor to Fielding's Bow Street Police Station.

The two theatres have long since ceased to be rivals. The Royal Opera House is now the official home of music and the dance. There are exceptions—benefits, Charity matinees and special occasions like the great Reinhardt production of *Oedipus*; but there are no more *Bluebeards*, no more *Babes in the Woods*, no more 'barbarous treatment of legitimate drama sacrificed to the pantomime'.

This quotation comes from *The Annals of Covent Garden Theatre* published nearly sixty years ago. But in spite of the author's enthusiasm for his subject his comment on the treatment of opera at Christmas time is surprisingly Philistine. He says that the librettist, Planché, 'had no real ground for complaint. He had no doubt been liberally paid . . . and the two entrepreneurs were simply following a well-established custom, etc.' As late as 1906, it seems, a work of art had no rights of its own. It is amusing to compare the point of view with a contemporary critic's comment which Brecht quotes just half a century later:

'A work of art is a living creature, and its maker, who will not permit it to be maimed, is in the right ten times over.'

However, in 1887 the ghost of Harlequin Lun was finally exorcised: an ungrateful business seeing that—as plain John Rich—he built the first house. *Jack and the*

Beanstalk was the last regular pantomime ever seen in the Theatre Royal Covent Garden.

The policy at Drury Lane is less assured. Pantomime continued there for many years. As a child I watched Dan Leno playing a fireman and singing his plaintive song of defeat.

> 'Off we go to answer duty's call.
> But when we get to the fire, the fire's gone out
> Or it hasn't been there at all.'

He made me feel very sorry for him; for he had a face like a mournful monkey. I couldn't bear the roars of laughter that greeted every line. I believed intensely in his troubles and I worried over him. Dear Dan Leno!

Since the last war Drury Lane has become the home of the big American musicals; but sometimes there is still Shakespeare. Only six years ago John Gielgud's voice was rolling Prospero's farewell across the huge auditorium as effortlessly as Neptune rolls his combers up a beach, so that going out one said: 'Why bother about the South Bank? Here we have already a National Theatre.' But the long queue already forming at the box-office was not booking for the next performance or even for a coming Shakespeare production. It was securing seats for the newly announced musical, *My Fair Lady*, and booking not for the next Christmas but for the Christmas after that.

But at least *My Fair Lady* paid a magnificent tribute to the Garden, and the librettists did better by Shaw than Dryden and Davenant did by Shakespeare. The story and the dialogue were used to the last inch, and the sets made one homesick. So did Stanley Holloway when he came on in the market scenes to sing 'A Little Bit of Luck'. To watch Holloway play the Dustman was to watch the spirit of the British Music Hall rising again. The performance was a salute to half a century of great comics from Arthur Roberts and George Robey to Sid Field.

B   33

I once sat next to Mr Field at a dinner-party. It was in Hollywood. Mr Chaplin had given it in his honour, and sat at the head of his long table looking demure, but gave an occasional inquisitive glance down the table as if wondering what his guest was discussing with such shining enthusiasm. As it happened, Sid Field was talking about Charlie Chaplin.

He spent most of that dinner telling me how the older man had been his professional inspiration since he was a youngster, and explaining that being entertained in Charlie Chaplin's own house was the most staggering and satisfying event of his career.

'And I have *got* to tell him so before I leave, and I don't know how.'

But after dinner he tackled his host, and the two of them stood a little apart talking to each other. It was like seeing a boy who has just won a scholarship trying to say thank-you to his pleased but embarrassed coach, who for his part is trying to say: 'Nonsense! It's all your own doing, and I'm proud of you.'

They both conveyed what they had to say by looks, a gesture, smiles, shrugs. There were very few words, and they were quite unaware that anyone was watching.

But I swear that behind them, surrounded by his troop of rude mechanicals, Shakespeare stood and beamed upon them both.

II

Moving In

It was in Coronation year, 1911, that I first explored the Market. A cousin of mine out in one of the village suburbs was making a garden that spring, and a suitcase full of plants was a good excuse for turning up for breakfast. I lived in faraway Kensington, once also a village. It meant getting up early and walking most of the way; but I had recently come upon Steele's account of how he did the same thing in 1712, and I wanted to compare notes.

'I lay one night at Richmond,' he says, 'and being restless, not out of dissatisfaction but out of a certain busy inclination one sometimes has, I rose at four in the morning and took boat for London. . . . We soon fell in with a fleet of gardeners. . . . It was the most pleasing scene imaginable to see the cheerfulness with which those industrious people plied their way to a certain sale of their goods. . . . The banks on each side are beautified with as agreeable plantations as any spot on earth; but the Thames itself, loaded with the product of each shore, added very much to the landskip. . . . I landed with ten sail of apricock boats at Strand Bridge, after having put in at Nine Elms and taken in melons. . . . I could not believe any place more entertaining than Covent Garden where I strolled from one fruitshop to another with crowds of agreeable young women about me who were purchasing fruit for their respective families.'

Such a river trip is still possible. A friend of mine has a house near Isleworth, so close to the Thames that the swans clamber on to the terrace and peck impatiently at her windows expecting, and getting, tit-bits; while huge barges still pass within hail, scattering the cormorants, gulls, ducks and divers. These barges still turn just above the weir and labour back; but they carry unknown cargoes. The fruit-boats no longer ply.

The walk from Kensington to the Market was a pleasant one fifty years ago, through a West End that has all but vanished. Hyde Park Corner had a feel of Waterloo about it: the great Duke's statue snorted at the Edwardian passer-by: 'We must never be beat! What will they say in England?' Mrs Alfred Lyttleton, whom I adored when I was young, once told me that she had seen the spectre of the Duke of Wellington climb the Piccadilly slope to Hyde Park Corner and disappear into Apsley House. She told it soberly as a fact, odd certainly, but certainly a fact.

But in the 'twenties the cement guns of the 1914 War Memorial took over the centre of the stage, and today the vast wheel of converging roads have made nonsense of the name. It is no more a corner than the Mall is a place to play pell-mell in.

Indeed the whole journey from Hyde Park Corner to Covent Garden is a record of change and loss. Piccadilly has been robbed of Devonshire House with its long wall and its air of peaceful grandeur, and nobody dreams today that Regent Street was once as elegant as a greyhound. Hamptons, west of the National Gallery, where everyone went for furnishings, was burnt to the ground in the last war. The National Gallery has been enlarged. Morley's, that beautiful old hotel on the east side of Trafalgar Square, was pulled down to make way for Africa House. The entrance to Charing Cross Station is no longer as cramped as it was in the day when my grandfather drove up daily to his office in a dogcart from 'pretty little Bow'. The Strand is widened, the Tivoli music-hall and the Cecil Hotel have been swept away, and a house in Southampton Street is no longer suitable for an actress like Mrs Oldfield who needs to sleep late after enchanting audiences at Drury Lane.

Southampton Street—a second Bedford in old maps—leaves the Strand nearly opposite the Savoy. It slopes up towards the Market past Maiden Lane, which is on its left. On the right comes Tavistock Street, a one-sided as well as a one-way road; for a market building now occupies the site of famous Tavistock Row. Then comes the alley that the Market calls 'The Private Roadway', which leads to the Central Market buildings. These went up in 1830, big halls with a central arcade—the Grand Avenue, the Central Row, its names are many—with shops and upper rooms. North and south are market halls, originally called the Long and the Apple market. These are filled with wire cages to hold produce, and there are two through-ways. The whole strange, clumsy but attractive oblong is surrounded by a portico and walk into which the bundles of vegetables are apt to overflow and are sometimes left over the weekend. They smell to heaven in hot weather, and cats and stray dogs find them useful.

But the surrounding brick cobbles are kept well washed. The market on a Sunday morning, clean and empty under a sky of driving clouds, is a delightful spectacle, like an early morning beach in summer, when the tide has left the sands smooth and the shingle a luminous amber after its submersion. It is exhilarating to stroll under the porticoes and through the empty markets, say hullo to, so to speak, one's occasional fellow-bathers, and end by diving into the Henrietta Street tunnel to the churchyard and so, with Pepys, to morning service and a drive into the country: Clapham or Islington for him, Midhurst for me. And Midhurst is also affiliated to the Garden, for Otway was a boy at Woolbeding, his plays were put on in Davenant's theatre in Lincoln's Inn, and he lies a stone's throw from the Market at St Clement Danes. As for Midhurst itself, Laurence Irving once showed me a letter written to his grandfather by Kean's nephew, giving chapter and verse for the interesting fact that while Kean's mother and sister were playing at Midhurst there arrived a letter from Kean telling them of his triumphant opening at Drury Lane, enclosing two five pound notes and promising his mother a

pound a week for life—a handsome pension in those days.
The nephew's letter is dated 1886, and it indignantly
denies rumours that 'my poor grandmother, sincerely
loved, I may say adored,' was not a good mother to Kean.

To the east of the Private Roadway—grand name for
a narrow alley—stand the three halls of the Flower Market
facing the top of Burleigh Street, which is the ideal spot
from which to watch the Strand processions go by.

The first of these three Halls is now an unpacking-
shed. The third has its entrance in Wellington Street, and
here the plants are sold. Between and connected with both
lies the great hall which houses the cut flowers and makes a
summer all the year round; though the blaze of colour is
nothing like as marvellous as it used to be. For most of the
flowers are now neatly boxed, and one misses the cottage-
bunches that used to be on sale, stuck in jam-jars or hung
from hooks at the sides of the stalls, such 'laughing flowers'
as Thomas Gray bought himself in hot July weather two
hundred years ago.

'My nosegays from Covent Garden consisted of nothing but
scarlet martagons, everlasting-peas, double stocks, pinks and
flowering marjoram.'

Marjoram must once have been extremely popular. Dryden said that sweet marjoram was the proper English name
for the flower which Venus heaped over the bed of Cupid,
but that he could not use it, 'for those village words, as I
may call them, give us a mean idea of the thing . . . the
sound of the Latin is so much more pleasing, by the just
mixture of the vowels with the consonants, that it raises
our fancies to conceive somewhat more noble than a
common herb, and to spread roses under him, and strew
lilies over him; a bed not unworthy the grandson of the
goddess.' Sweet flowering marjoram is not a common herb
in London shops today. Everlasting peas would scarcely be
worth transport; but pinks and double-stocks still have a
ready sale. So do lilies-of-the-valley grown in the open, and

38

the wild primroses that the children pick, short-stalked and tied with cotton. But not many wild-flowers are seen nowadays in the Market.

After those Edwardian visits I forgot the Garden till the First World War was behind us and we were well into the 'twenties. By then life had changed for me. I had left the stage and begun to write novels. Then came a play, which led to a farm in Devonshire; but I had to have room to keep the elaborate evening-dresses and cloaks of the nineteen-twenties, and I had to sleep somewhere when I came to London on business; so I was looking for a lodging.

My publisher's office was in Bedford Street, and after a visit I used to cross the road into Henrietta Street to McNamara's, that small stationer which every journalist and market-man in Covent Garden depends upon, and there I used to load up; for nothing more helps the beginning of a new novel than a wildly extravagant purchase of pens, ink and paper. You never use any of it. You scribble on envelopes and backs of articles and up the sides and round the tops of pages which are supposed to be typed and done with; but a visit to McNamara started one off.

Then I used to cross back to No. 6 where the Curtis Brown agency was established. I looked forward to that visit. Agencies were personal, friendly places in the 'twenties, and the heads of the Curtis Brown departments were as young as I was, and we were all building our careers. Michael Joseph, Anthony Richardson, Laurence Pollinger, Olwen Bowen—how young and hopeful we were! As for C.B. himself, he was everyone's friend and father confessor.

'Mr Curtis Brown, I hardly like to tell you, but I'm trying to write a play about Shakespeare.'

'Well my dear, sometimes the big theme lifts the writer. Not that it will sell.'

Curtis Brown's had another attraction. Everyone at the office firmly believed that Jane Austen used to stay at Number 6 when she visited her brother, who was manager of the bank next door. Proof positive—Barclay's had the ground floor of Number 5. Vain to point out that the official address was Number 10. 'Numbers get changed.'

So the Magazine Department continued to keep its stacks of manuscripts modestly but obstinately in 'Jane Austen's fireplace'; though I could never find any account of that fireplace when I looked up her letters. But I soon found out that nearly every door or once-door in the street was linked with the name of a writer or a painter or a poet.

Have you ever read any piece by Hannah More? I haven't, and yet she is a very vivid person to me. Johnson snubbed her and Walpole teased her; but each counted her a friend, and David Garrick and his wife insisted that she should come and live with them, which she did, and was once heard to praise Garrick for his tact. She said that he had never, except on two occasions and that by accident, allowed her to meet any of his fellow professionals. It looks as if she were a formidable Miss Prim, but she was undeniably a personage. She believed in education, she fought the battles of the poor and the ignorant, she was capable of appreciating greater minds than her own. Prim and much concerned about morality, she had an incongruously broad sense of fun. She tells the story against herself of being carried through Covent Garden during savage election riots by sulky chairmen who wouldn't listen to her and wouldn't put her down. The average maiden lady shut up in a sedan-chair might well be scared; but Hannah More was not too scared to laugh.

Miss More and Miss Austen are but two of the women whose names brighten Henrietta Street. Miss Kelly lived at Number 8—Fanny Kelly, the brilliant actress whom Charles Lamb wanted to marry. Kitty Clive, Garrick's leading lady for twenty years, was another inhabitant of that starry street, and let us remember without surprise that she simply hated Hannah More.

Earlier still Samuel Cooper, the great 'limner in little', had a studio in the street. There Pepys visited him and

saw the miniature of Frances Stuart, the lovely woman
who refused King Charles. We know her face well—on
our pennies—'and a pretty thing it is,' says Pepys in a
flurry of admiration, 'that the King chose her face to
represent Britannia by.' Pepys, much impressed by the
miniature, decided that his own beautiful wife should be
painted by Cooper, and fussed in and out to his heart's
content while the sittings were going on. He was not
perfectly satisfied with the result—there was something
not quite right about the dress and the complexion—but
Cooper was the fashion, and at least it was a most rare
piece of work, as to the painting.

The writers, painters and actors who had lived in
Henrietta Street made it glamorous anyway; but to a young
author in the nineteen-twenties it had another charm—
its publishers. Macmillans, Duckworths, Pearsons, Bohn
Père (we owe the blessed cheap editions to his son in
once-York Street), Williams and Norgate, Chapman and
Hall have all inhabited Henrietta Street, and Heinemann's
of the distinguished little windmill used to look across to
the churchyard of St Paul's, Covent Garden from a meek
doorway in Bedford Street. The air of Henrietta Street was
heady with contracts and dreams.

As I came out of Number 6 that morning I thought to
myself that to live in it or near it would be the luckiest
thing that could ever happen to anyone who wanted the life
literary, the life artistic or the life theatrical. I had had a
taste of all three, and longed for more. But of course one
couldn't possibly hope to get a flat or even a couple of
rooms in that pre-empted street. A pity!

Then, as I paused at the top of Southampton Street,
the Garden itself, like an old friend half forgotten, came
rushing at me in terms of noise, colour, movement, the
smell of greenery and citrus, the slow insolence of pigeons
and the flickering passage here and there of a half-wild
Garden cat.

It was a revealing moment, like coming in to the gallery

41

to watch the last act of a show one had seen once before, carelessly, and thinking with a sense of shock: 'Why didn't I realise sooner what a great play this is?'

Then I thought of Dickens 'staring at the pineapples'.

Suddenly I said to myself: 'This is where I am going to live.'

It was meant. I looked along Tavistock Street, and directly ahead there hung out from a first-floor window over the usual market frontage a sign which said: 'Offices to Let'. Two youngsters were just putting up the shutters.

I went in and talked to the men in charge of the boxes and buckets of flowers. They called the owner. I soon learned that he was a duke of the carnation world; but it was years before I learned, and then not from him, that he was an M.C. of the First World War, and also that he had at the time emptied his glass-houses of his whole capital treasure of carnations, in order to grow war-time vegetables. Then came the second war and a second throwing out of irreplaceable specimens. The war took more than that from him: it took his brilliant son. But in 1924 we all believed that the war to end war had done its job, and that we could all afford to plan for a pleasant future.

He came in, a friendly countryman, and we eyed each other.

'I saw the notice over the first-floor window—"Offices to Let".'

'That's right.'

'Only offices? Or could one sleep there?'

Everyone roared with laughter.

'Think of the noise!' said Dallow.

'I could sleep at the back.'

'Dirtiest place in London,' said Harry.

'It's worse in Chelsea. I have friends there.'

Len spoke up. 'But Miss, you couldn't get out of the house in the morning, not with luggage. Taxis can't get through ever.'

'I should only have a suitcase. I could carry it to the Strand.'

Then Brian, the foreman, faced me, for my own sake, with the unarguable. 'There are rats,' he said.

But when the owner saw that I was in earnest he took me along the dark passage to the foot of the grubby stairs with the beautiful curving hand-rail. There was no door beyond the general one to the street, and a private entrance, he told me at once, was impossible; for the porter and his wife lived in the attic, and the manager slept on the second floor. But if I still wanted to look over the first floor pair—?

I did.

'This way, then!'

The eighteenth-century rooms were in a desolate state, with soot and a long-dead fire spilling out over the dirty oaken floorboards. These polished well later on. Two huge sash-windows looked directly across to the Covered Way and past the Private Road to the sparkling glass roof of the Floral Hall. The bedroom was dark, and the tiny powder-room had an immense fireplace which would have to be pulled out; but the rooms had a charm for me, and I took them at once. My new landlord collaborated generously over repairs, and in two months I was settled in with clean paint, a bathroom, bookshelves, desk, a big bunch of carnations and anything else that could keep a writer happy. True, I had no front door. Against that I had the thing I enjoyed most—the easiest possible access to Drury Lane, Covent Garden, the Aldwych, the Strand, the Stoll, the Gaiety, the Tivoli, the Adelphi, the Vaudeville, the Savoy, the Duke of York's, the Coliseum, Prince's, the Winter Garden, the Phoenix, and later the Fortune and the Duchess. I also had a stall front row in the best theatre of all—the Garden itself.

From the window looking left I could see Garrick's house facing the Market, its frontage as neat and demure as the face of Garrick himself hesitating between the

Tragic and the Comic Muse in Reynolds's droll portrait-fantasy. Next door is 'French's', where the amateurs still buy acting editions of the new plays—comedies preferred—with all the 'props' in neat lists and all the business in stage-shorthand: 'Down L. Move up C. Goes off R.' Then comes the shallow-stepped, spacious entry to Boulestin's, the underground restaurant.

The story of Boulestin's death in Paris during the Second War is a sad one; but the restaurant is faithful to his memory and his fine cooking. The cocktail parlour is an innovation; but otherwise it is just as it always was with tall, curtained windows that never open on daylight, Rembrandt-brown walls, and a vast electric fan at the far end of the main room. I know every click of that fan. For a week or two towards the end of the last war we had a fly-bomb phase, and during it one was supposed to stay below ground-level. So I used to come across from Tavistock Street after the restaurant closed and sleep on one of the banques with that fan blowing fiercely down the back of my neck. Every night I'd find a clean tablecloth laid ready on the narrow seat, a minute glass of Kirsch on the table for me and a bowl of water on the floor for my dog—a welcome from the house. That was a shelter to be grateful for, a kind place run by kind people.

Beyond Boulestin's, again just visible from first-floor windows and plainly from the attic, was the roof of St Paul's, Covent Garden, the actors' church, looking more or less as it looks, reversed, in the Hogarth print, *Morning*. North lay what was left of the Piazza; but the east end with all its associations, comforts and beauties was pulled down a hundred years ago to make room for the Floral Hall. This is a construction in glass and steel left over, the Market people say, from the 1851 Exhibition in Hyde Park when it was transferred to Sydenham and became the Crystal Palace. The Victorians had their own sense of the poetic—a crystal palace exactly described that fantastic Victorian erection. As children we used to see it

44

from the North Downs glittering across the valley, looking like something out of a fairytale, and in later childhood it was my playground. So the Floral Hall, seen from Tavistock Street, was a welcome-home.

The Floral Hall opened in 1860 with a Volunteer Ball, and in a print of the time the interior is as pretty as a pantomime transformation-scene. The exterior used to look exactly like a vast greenhouse, and on summer afternoons the palm-like fan-frontage and shimmering glass panes did really suggest coolness and a garden.

> 'The garden glasses shone, and momently
> The twinkling laurel scattered silver lights.'

That was the effect. It took the eye. I had a studio in the Tavistock Street house and kept a couple of spare easels for friends: and nearly everyone of them tried to paint the Floral Hall.

But in 1940 all the glass was smashed by flack, and when the roof was repaired it was painted green. There was a crow's nest on the roof of the Opera House where a sentinel watched over the Market during the war; but the Floral Hall hid the parent building, and it looked as if the crow's nest were part of the green-roofed conservatory. Then in 1956 one of the Garden's many fires broke out, and the whole roof of the Floral Hall went up in flames. It has since been replaced by a conventional sloping roof, glassed, and now the Opera House can once more be seen behind it.

The new roof is but one of a hundred changes. Petrol-driven vans have replaced most of the dray-horses: the porters no longer stroll across the paving-stone cobbles carrying on their heads eight or ten wicker-baskets balanced on each other like stacked cones in an ice-cream shop. The last one I ever saw had become a waste-paper basket in the vestry of the Garden church.

But in the 'thirties the baskets were as familiar a sight as Davenant's gipsies and as little changed since his day.

45

The handsome, swarthy men with their painted carts and their small, adroit ponies waved their whips like flags of Bohemia and Illyria, and there was no escaping their eloquent women. But it was worth crossing a palm with silver to see intelligence, sharp as a jackdaw's grey eye, summing up the client and deciding what sort of future would be suitable before beginning to 'mark and foretell happy events of love'.

But the gipsies are going, going, gone with the lavender-criers and the Italian ribbon-sellers who moved like scarecrows through the traffic with scarves and ribbons draped over their rigidly outstretched arms. Gone too is the muffin-man with his basket and his green baize apron who used to cut across the Garden every Sunday afternoon ringing his evocative bell.

> 'Oh, who has seen the muffin-man,
> The muffin-man, the muffin-man?
> Has anybody seen the muffin-man
> Who lives in Crumpet Lane?'

That is one of the many nursery-rhymes which is gibberish to a child of the nineteen-sixties. But to late Victorians it evoked a picture as vivid as a Tissot—the empty street, the Sabbath gloom and the reactions of faces at top-floor windows to the bell that was so cheerily not a church-bell.

When the Lunts were in London playing in *The Visitor* I called on them one Sunday afternoon at the Savoy. They were watching the autumn mists swirling up over the Embankment Gardens, and Alfred came to meet me with the tragic cry: 'What has happened to the muffin-man?' Muffins and crumpets meant London, and he wanted some for tea—crumpets for choice—but he had searched the Strand shops in vain.

I found, when I continued the search next day, that there is a tide in the affairs of muffins and crumpets. They are never on sale till winter has set in. Fortunately their season began before *The Visitor* closed. Anyway they are

easy enough to make—see Mrs Beeton, the 1888 edition.
At least muffins are easy to make, for I have made them.
But for crumpets special moulds are needed, and I have
never come across one yet. It heads the list of useful
articles that the Victorians had and we haven't—double
knife-cleaners, slop-pails with strawbound handles, rotten-
stone, tinder-boxes, a great, vast, roomy wicker cage to
house a bird with a temporarily damaged wing, paint-
brushes that are resilient after washing, foot-warmers and
half-curtained beds. Indeed the Victorians understood comfort. Stainless knives don't cut like Victorian steel, and
Hoovers don't freshen up a carpet as tea-leaves and elbow-
grease used to do. As for pressure-cookers, they are nothing
new.

A year or two ago I was shown at a Sussex ironmonger's
a most delectable pressure-cooker, right size, right shape,
exactly what I had been hunting for. But it was not for
sale.

'You see ma'am, it's discontinued stock.'

It turned out that the cooker, like the firm, dated from
the year 1700, and had survived at the back of an over-
crowded shelf for two hundred and sixty odd years.

So I still have hopes of tracking down a crumpet-
mould; for muffins and crumpets are as old as the cooker.
When the abominable Peter Pindar is trying to be rude to
George III and his Queen he sneers at them for enjoying a
muffin with their hyson—their cup of tea.

'Now at their ease, the cares of dinner past,
Great George and Charlotte hyson's liquid taste.
Three beauteous princesses adorn the board;
Three toasted muffins show a princely lord.'

This is quoted merely for the sake of the muffins; for
Peter Pindar is so hateful that one resents his having lived
in the Garden, even in a Tavistock Row garret. He repre-
sents that passion for abuse which was the besetting sin
of the Garden wits; though Johnson, who lived through

47

the phase, shrugs it off as unimportant. 'Abuse is not so dangerous when there is no vehicle of wit and delicacy, no subtle conveyance. . . . The difference between coarse and refined abuse is as the difference between being bruised by a club and wounded by a poisoned arrow—' which more or less settles the hash of Peter Pindar.

At any rate his type of abuse has died out in the Garden. If you sit at a first-floor window in fantastic Tavistock Street the exchanges heard below are certainly uninhibited. There is plenty of rough language; but hatefully malicious language, no. 'Brother' is still a fairly common form of address, and the main characteristic is a mustn't-grumble mood, even when things are going well. When there is serious trouble, of course, everyone perks up, delighted and delightful.

That I found out when the last war broke. I had been warned by our street Warden that it was my duty as occupier to see that everyone in the house went down to the cellar when the siren sounded. But could I get the men down into the cellar? They were amenable enough when I called. They came politely down the ladder into that queer retreat with its smell of rats and roses and its flowers standing in pails all over the damp bricks; but they wouldn't *stay* down. I would turn my back to soothe the porter's frightened old grandmother, and instantly Harry and Ralph and even Brian the grave foreman were nipping up the ladder again and out into the street, where they stood watching the sky, fascinated and completely fearless.

The Garden never cared to be put out of its way by Hitler. One morning after a particularly noisy night I passed the wholesale flower-shop on the corner. The display-vase in the centre of the window had no flowers; but it was not empty. A porter's cap was fitted neatly on the wire flower-holder, and 'Business as Usual' was scrawled on a card and propped in front.

That's the Garden.

Another eccentricity is the Market habitué's complete disregard of traffic. The barrow-boys take precedence as a matter of course, and the morning buyers skitter across the narrow gaps between lorry and lorry like water-beetles crossing a pond, and the old hands who crouch in the gutter are hard to move as they furtively pick-over broken-stalked marguerites and wilted carnations. Later they wipe clean the faces of the flowers, scissor the petals, wire the heads and then make buttonholes out of their loot to sell at street-corners.

My home was exactly opposite the Covered Way. Its vast green door used to be rolled up at night like a Brob-dingnagian blind. The Market opened earlier in the 'thirties, which made it harder to fall asleep, so I used often to come through to the front room and settle down on the sofa to watch the play till I drowsed off—watch and listen, for conversation rose free and unfettered from the street below as the lorries lurched in to unload. That custom has ended, they tell me; but in my time porters took down the boxes from the lorries and unpacked in odd corners till the place was a blaze of colour under the electric lights. The scene was even more beautiful when the sun rose and the un-needed lights dimmed.

Sometimes the view would be suddenly blocked by a cheerful face grinning in at me—Len, standing level with my window on the top of his lorry-load of boxes. Len would lift box after box from the top of the pile and throw them down in turn to his mate on the pavement, checking as he threw. 'One daff—two daffs—one violets—walls—walls—walls . . .'—one soon learnt what would be good cheap next morning. Long after I had gone back to bed I'd hear the boxes being dumped into the shop and passed on down the ladder to the cellar. Thump, thump, dollop, thump! It went on for hours.

All the lorries on the south side of the Garden had to pass the teller in Burleigh Street. The teller in the nineteen-thirties was a cheerful little woman of sixty, neat, rosy and

49

buttoned-up against the cold all the year round. She
arrived soon after midnight and stood till the Market
closed on the pavement outside the Lyceum stage door,
checking the drivers. She had absolute authority and was
never disobeyed; for she had once been a housemaid in a
great Edwardian mansion, and she still had the manner of
her training. Everyone knew her; she knew everyone. She
never forgot a face and she never missed a new hat nor a
torn hem. Dear h'Esther! She is dead now; but she is still
part of the Garden.

The years went by, from the early 'twenties up to the
war when I got my front-door at last, and on till the middle
'fifties, and all the while I had been getting an education
that money could not buy, for living in the Market it was
inevitable that I should want to find out more about it.
Somebody told me that Kean had once lived in my rooms;
so I had to read everything ever written about Kean. An
old gentleman in the Flower Hall introduced himself one
day as Paxton's nephew; so then I had to get hold of Miss
Markham's biography of her grandfather, and that led to
looking up the biographies of all the people he in turn had
known, and the Victorians led back to the Regency, and
back—and back—till I was in the Elizabethan age, and
Covent Garden was a meadow again. Fine, confused
feeding, and God bless the London Library!

After a while I also found out that living in the Market
had a queer effect on one's sense of period. It must be that
time is unstable in any district where opposites meet as
they do in the Garden: country and town, commerce and
romance, art and cabbages, magic and money, not to
speak of past and future. Indeed, I wonder if any other
plot of ground in the world, except perhaps the Forum
in Rome, gives the passer-by such a happy sense of being
alive at one and the same moment in all periods of a city's
history, or of being jostled by crowds of invisibles who
share the Garden with you. They co-exist with you. They
prickle on your skin like electric sparks on a frosty morning

as they pass you, alive in their own time-space and busy on their own important lively affairs.

Look—I go along Maiden Lane to buy angelica at the herb-shop, which incidentally has been established there for over a hundred years. A sixteenth-century herbalist once marketed his wares in the south-west corner of the Market, and by 1735 the enterprise had become a big business. Then it was taken over by a City firm. But one of the former staff, a certain Richard Brooks, set up for himself in Maiden Lane, and his shop still sells herbs and all the spices of Arabia as well as the angelica and crystal-lised cherries which I need to decorate my cake. I stroll westward, working out how much I shall need, and sud-denly another part of me is conscious that I am sharing the street with three gentlemen. We stroll along side by side without disturbing each other. Then, as I pass by, a front-door wavers and mixes into the sign of the White Peruke, and the three gentlemen pause, indifferent alike to me and to the stream of one-way taxis. They are enquiring of the hair-dresser if his lodger is at home—a French gentleman.

The hair-dresser, who is French himself, hesitates. Then he gets the idea.

'Monsieur de Voltaire?'

'Monsieur de Voltaire.'

'Ah yes, he is just come in. And the gentlemen's names?'

'Mr Young, Mr John Gay, Mr Alexander Pope.'

Monsieur de Voltaire is in his private sitting-room on the first floor, writing—what? Letters concerning the English, probably, or he might be deep in the civil wars of France; but his visitors are none the less welcome, specially the dwarfish gentleman with the large eyes and pain-twisted countenance; for Mr Alexander Pope, in Monsieur de Voltaire's opinion, is 'the most elegant, the most correct poet and at the same time the most harmonious that England ever gave birth to.' So they are begged to step up, though it will break still further into his morning. It seems that he has just returned from a call on Mr

51

Congreve who, again in Monsieur de Voltaire's opinion, 'has raised the glory of comedy to a greater height than any English writer before or since his time.' Nevertheless the visit has not been altogether a success.

'He spoke of his works as of trifles that were beneath him; and hinted to me that I should visit him on no other foot than that of a gentleman. . . . I answered, that had he been so unfortunate as to be a mere gentleman I should never have come to see him . . . and I was very much disgusted at so unseasonable piece of vanity.'

There are chuckles, and Pope has something to say about the Ruling Passion; but I cannot wait to hear it. I have to buy my angelica. When I get back, though, I shall look up Edmund Gosse's book on Congreve; for I seem to remember that he has put up a brilliant defence of Congreve's alleged vanity, and Edmund Gosse is another of the gods. If someone had told me in 1912 that in ten years' time I should go down to dinner on his arm I should have thought them quite mad, as mad as if they had told me that I should one day talk to Sarah Bernhardt herself on the stage of the Lyceum.

But that also happened. She was in a wheel-chair, a skull with burning eyes. Her voice was a whisper. She was frail as paper, but with a charm like—like stephanotis.

It is not only the gods who linger in the Garden. Poor old John—'Punch', the Market called him—died years ago; but I can't pass the fruit-barrow at the foot of Burleigh Street without getting the feel of him still. He sits on a dustbin, just as he did when we ate cherries together in the leisurely 'thirties and discussed boot-leather and Rowton House lodgings and his niece in the country, and that wearing pain in his leg.

I know what I'm talking about. I lived in the Garden for thirty years, and I'm recording not a sentimental wish but an impression that has grown with time into a conviction. The Garden is as enduring in its collective life as a beehive or a tribe, or a play by Shakespeare. It makes and obeys its own laws and is swayed by private moods. It asserts itself through an individual at one moment, at another through the movement of its crowds.

There are Sunday mornings when the Garden remembers its youth and is as pleasant as a country field. Then sheep graze once more in the Long Acre, and the youngsters engage in the football war, while in a far corner someone is planting out rows of the new-fangled salads that Queen Catherine of Aragon brought with her from Spain. At other times the Garden is all rollicking Victorianism. But the atmosphere can also be, suddenly, thick with a stale, cabbagy smell of yesterday's poverties that catches the throat. Then strangers say: 'The fogs are bad this autumn.' But it isn't only the fogs. The Garden has a random pulse, and when that quickens its past overflows into its present and has an effect on all who live there whether they know it or not. Its effect on me was to make me bless the day that I moved in. I was in luck, and I knew it.

I only discovered the full extent of my luck, however, when I came home one evening after a heavy day's work in the studios, with only twenty minutes to spare and tickets for the Ballet. I found then that I could bathe, change, leave the house at five minutes before the hour, cut up the Private Road and across the Market, along Russell Street, turn up Bow Street and be in the entrance-hall, showing my tickets, a full two minutes before the show began.

'Round to the left and along the foyer. You'll have to be quick, madam, but I think you'll just do it.'

Round to the left past the coffee-bar and the Ladies' Room, up the side staircase by the orchestra, pause an instant, beaten back by the blaze of bright lights, crimson and gold hangings and pink faces, slip into the last seat of the second row—click—subside—madam just does it.

The lights go down.

The silence lengthens.

The first note sounds.

53

III

The Bedford Street Entrance

As you walk up the Bedford Street hill from the Strand you have on your left an enormously long frontage, part shop-window, part brick-wall, which young people call the Civil Service Stores. But old people call it the 'new' Civil Service Stores; for in the early 'nineties the main store was in the City.

It was the Selfridges of the age. Small children who lived in the country and were taken to London for a day's refurbishing always ended up in Queen Victoria Street. Breakfast was at six-thirty. Then came a three-mile drive to the station behind two young horses, imperfectly under my father's control: Hammond the coachman sat beside him and chafed. The City train left at eight o'clock, and on the way up to Cannon Street, third class—first class was sacred to male parents—the tedium of the journey was relieved by watching for the Dog-Man.

The Dog-Man was the decade's most sensational effort at publicity. Most advertisements knew their meek place at the end of the Victorian era. The most daring was the Pears' Soap picture of the dirty tramp writing his testimonial: 'Two years ago I used your soap. Since then I used no other.' There was also the Mellin's Food baby, the rhymed Waverley Pen advertisement, the Mazawattee Tea ladies dressed as England, Scotland and Ireland, and a few other such demure efforts to attract attention to worthwhile goods. But there was one superb, exhibitionist gesture. It was better than Shell, better than Schweppes. It was made by Spratt's Dog Biscuits.

Near New Cross the railway-line ran along a sort of

fly-over with the London landscape lying below. As the train drew across, the head of a St Bernard dog, three times life-size, rose up from behind the parapet, and as the coaches joggled slowly past the head bowed affably and the jaws moved in a welcoming bark. Then, just before the rails curved the carriages away, that St Bernard dog used to take off his head and, holding it in his hand, turn into a meek servant of the company bowing for the last time as we disappeared. The excitement held till Cannon Street and was the happy prologue to the day's adventures —the dentist, the office, the Old Civil Service, the treat.

The dentist was a fearful business. There were no local injections in those days, and lamentations were not encouraged. One endured—and got half-a-crown out of it. Then came the visit to the partners' room of the parental office in St Mary Axe—dark green walls, a turkey carpet and gas-brackets, yellow satin-wood bookcases with green Liberty silk gathered behind the glass. The two sacred desks, looking like piano-playing machines, were set back to back so that my father and his partner could face each other with mutual irritation at every crisis of their day. The inner offices always had a red-hot coal fire burning in the large, elegant grate, and in recesses on either side of the mantelpiece hung portraits of the two Founders, the senior partner who was knighted and my grandfather who wasn't.

The outer offices were even more agreeable: there were tins of biscuits, and the rooms smelt pleasantly of pipes and quires of writing-paper with a surface like a good motor-road. There were no typewriters and no females— many conferences were to be held between the aunts and my father before the first girl typist was risked; but the elderly clerks were friends. We knew their grandchildren by name and used to write them picture-letters on blue-lined foolscap sheets. There were treasures to be fished out of the high desks—clips, ends of sealingwax, discarded pen-nibs that didn't suit old-fashioned copperplate handwriting, and once my grandfather produced a small, highly polished green leather purse with forty threepenny-bits in it. He had saved them for me—forty silver three-penny bits and one fourpenny bit for good measure. The visit to St Mary Axe more than made up for the visit to the dentist.

Next came early lunch at a dark little chop-house in a paved city alley with posts at either end. The meal was served in wooden compartments. Lobsters occurred. There was sand on the floor and it got into one's high boots through the lacings and had to be shaken out.

After lunch—a hansom with one aunt and two children squeezed into the double seat, and the apron doors closed over everyone's knees. A trap in the roof opened, and there was a cabby's face looking down and hoarsely whispering. There followed the jingling drive to 'the dear old Civil Service Stores'.

Membership tickets had to be shown before shopping could begin, and as the current aunt had nearly always forgotten them there was generally a guilty interview with a floor-walker and a wait. Then came a grim hour of trying-on kid-gloves that pinched the wrist in the buttoning season, Greenaway bonnets that rendered the wearer stone deaf, and reefer jackets too tight round the armholes, a navy one for everyday and a scarlet one for Sunday.

Then came ices, very pink, swallowed too quickly and making the stopped tooth jump. There was not much time left, and the treat was still to come.

The treat began with a bus-jaunt up Fleet Street and along the Strand to Charing Cross. Then, if it was my turn to choose, we went on past the old Morley Hotel to the National Gallery, because I had a passion for the Pesellino *Trinity* which hung in the big Italian saloon. It was the first picture after the entrance to the little side-room on the left. The Father's arms enclosed the Son on the Cross, and the Dove brooded over them. The picture entranced me, partly because of the colours, which were as gorgeous as our little nursemaid's Sunday dress of parma-violet serge trimmed with moss-green velvet; but still more because it gave me the solution to a problem that had worried me ever since I was first taken to church.

'And yet They are not three Gods, but one God.'

What did it mean? Was it a riddle?

But when I saw the Pesellino *Trinity* I knew exactly what it meant, or thought I did, and it was an immense relief to me. Because children can't express themselves coherently their inner lives are not necessarily incoherent. They have no yard-stick by which to measure the world in which they have awakened; but the power to feel is as violent at three as it is at thirty, and the need to reason controls it from the dawn of awareness, which comes pretty early, even though the memory of it may fade.

I happen to be memory-lucky. I clearly remember being shown my brother in long clothes when I was just over two. His face, his nurse, the room, the wallpaper—all is still neat in my mind. I vividly remember, too, what life was like in a country middle-class house at the time of the Matabele war, and how one heard words like 'impi' and 'kraal', and how one January evening as we sat on the hearthrug in front of the fire playing with the four new kittens, my father came home from the City saying that Lobengula was dead.

One mustn't generalize; but I remember my own childhood, and I am sure that awareness of life was stronger in it than at any other period; but the time-sense was different, and one hadn't learned the ropes. Why does nearly every teenager revolt? Because at last it has found out *how* to revolt. It always wanted to. Then in old age the situation is reversed. 'She used not to be so vain and greedy.' 'He wasn't always so tyrannical.'

Yes, she was. Yes, he was. It's the power to cope with life that is fading. Old men forget their training, and so do old women.

Of course education in the modern sense didn't exist

in the 'nineties, but reading was early acquired. My cousins and I were averagely intelligent, no more; but we all read for private entertainment by the time we were five. It wasn't precocity. It was lack of TV. In a sense the game of reading was our only education as small children, though our governess was good at botany and saw to it that we learnt by heart all the questions as well as the answers in *The Child's Guide to Knowledge*. That got me through a couple of B.B.C. Brains Trusts forty years later.

But training in thinking for oneself came, oddly enough, from having to go to church too often. Services were services in those days—Litany *and* Communion, followed, in my village, by a scholar's sermon. If a child didn't choose to listen the tedium became so unendurable that it fidgeted till it had to be taken out, which was a disgrace to be avoided.

So the child listened. Naturally it didn't know what the Rector was talking about; but the voice was clear, the pronunciation admirable, and the rhythms pleased the ear as good woodcarving pleases the eye, sternly. Bit by bit the ear was trained to absorb verbal shapes, and the mind to grapple with ideas. When the child heard that some of those ideas made sense to the man in the pulpit but that others emphatically didn't, it learned another valuable lesson. It learned that if it didn't think a thing was true it should say so.

The *Pilgrim's Progress* was allowed on Sundays, and the story itself was greatly enjoyed; but there was far too much about Hell in it. I was selfish and had a temper, and knew it; so the future torments of Hell haunted me as I went to sleep. Eternity, beginning where the stars end, was a frightful thought.

But those long, dry, reasoning sermons in the little twelfth-century church were a mental discipline, and at last the results showed. I still remember sitting up in bed one night and looking out across the garden to the snowball-tree on the lawn. It was hung with small white moons. Behind it a big white moon shone from a sky that was a bluish-slate, the exact colour of my favourite cousin's eyes. I looked, and I thought about burning for ever—and ever—and suddenly I said to myself: 'I don't believe a word of it.'

It was like coming out of a railway-tunnel. I slept well.

I don't suppose that many five-year-olds have to go through that particular tunnel today, and that is a gain. But neither do they experience quite so early the sense of power that comes from facing a problem and settling it, and that is a loss. I owed much to that learned little clergyman, who never dreamed that he was teaching a very small human being to use its common-sense.

He was an elderly man with a private tragedy of which I knew something—children hear all the gossip in a village. He died long before I grew up; but in the 'thirties I wrote a play called *Mariners*, thinking of him, though I changed the story. Lewis Casson played the part with Sybil Thorndike as his stage-wife, and he was exactly like his original. The real wife I only saw once, standing at the gate between stone walls and wearing a yellow mink tippet—mink was a despised fur in those days. Sybil Thorndike gave her a despairing, harsh beauty not easily forgotten.

Another educational factor in a middle-class 'nineties childhood was 'politics'. It is difficult to explain to the over-entertained world of today how the nursery craved for excitement, and how Westminster provided it. The Jameson raid was our introduction to drama. Lord Salisbury was the great father-figure, and Mr Balfour and Joseph Chamberlain were our Gary Coopers and Marlon Brandos.

Once I was taken to a meeting at the Cannon Street hotel to hear Mr Balfour speak. It was just after King Edward had come to the throne. Mr Balfour was very long and grey and faint, like a lightly-coloured lithograph, and his manner was gentle. During his speech he happened to refer to the King's prerogatives, and some lout at the back of the hall called out: 'Don't you say anything against the King!'

At that came a transformation. The speaker lit up—it was like a flame leaping up suddenly from grey coals— and obliterated the heckler in a couple of scorching sentences: and I knew at last what Lempriere's Classical Dictionary meant when it talked about Jupiter's thunderbolts.

As a quickener of the imagination that fat leatherbound Lempriere came next to the Bible and *The Pilgrim's Progress* for me. It belonged to my grandfather and I still possess it. But the story of childhood is written in a private language, and private languages have no business to be printed. They are only permissible if they recall a language that everyone used and places that everyone knew, like the toyshop place in the Strand, which must, I suppose, have been the Lowther Arcade, or how should I know the song so well?

'As I was walking down the Lowther Arcade,
    The place for children's toys,
Where you may purchase a dolly or a spade
    For your good little girls and boys,
And as I passed a certain stall
    A wee wee voice said to me:
"Oh, I am a soldier in a little tin hat
    And I ride on a tin gee-gee." '

A visit to the toyshop place was the alternative treat at the end of the bi-annual London outing. There my brother ran riot among steam-engines, clockwork trains and tin soldiers. After that there was a rush to catch the train at Charing Cross. My father met it at London Bridge, and we all went home together.

Victorian aunts were tough; but even they must have been thankful when the *new* dear old Civil Service Stores shortened the endurance test.

There were two Bedford Streets—the first is now

60

Southampton Street, and the lower half of the present Bedford Street was Half Moon Street in early maps. Our modern Bedford Street only began half-way up the hill. Today the Civil Service Stores occupies the west side of the street from the Strand to Chandos Place, and a flower-seller used to stand by the doorstep of the upper level exit in my time. His flowers were not of the freshest; but they had to be bought because he was a friend of Punch. Chandos Place used to be Chandos Street and was once spelt Chandois. It was at a Chandos Street inn that the Bow Street Runners captured the renowned highwayman, Claude Duval.

Duval was the romantic sensation of his day. He was a Norman Frenchman, born at Domfront, once the stronghold of our own Henry II, the first Plantagenet king. For centuries the town had a fighting history: which accounts, perhaps, for Claude Duval.

Duval came over to England in 1660 as a page to an English nobleman, and after various adventures turned highway robber in the *Beggar's Opera* style. He was a successful and popular one; for he was young and handsome, had delightful manners and treated the ladies he robbed with wheedling charm. Once, after persuading a flustered woman to dance with him on the heath, he restored a part of her property. Not the whole. He was gallant, but he was also a prudent Frenchman. There was great lamentation when he was caught. The whole town attended his execution and visited him afterwards as he 'lay in state' at a St Giles inn.

Opposite Chandos Place the road narrows into Maiden Lane, which leads to Southampton Street and the Market. The next turning on the east is Henrietta Street, which also leads to the Market, and a few doors higher up the road you come to a small flagged yard with private doorways on either wall—Inigo Place. Forty years ago a door on the right led to Edith Craig's flat where, on a lucky day, you might find her mother with her—Ellen Terry.

61

I hold in my mind a picture of Ellen Terry. I have many of her on the stage: Ellen Terry sitting on the edge of the table in the buck-basket scene with Tree and Mrs Kendall, and laughing till she laughed herself off the table and slid gracefully to the floor—Ellen Terry helping Captain Brassbound to find the armhole of his coat-sleeve —Ellen Terry as the statue at the end of *A Winter's Tale*, very slowly coming to life. But this picture is of Ellen Terry as an old woman, standing at the far end of a long room in Bedford Street, showing me her own portrait as a girl of sixteen. Her first husband, G. F. Watts, painted it and called it *Ophelia*. It is a very young, eager face. The old Ellen Terry as she leant forward unconsciously took up the same pose, and for a blazing moment there was no difference at all.

Another flat in the same block belonged to Ben Webster and his wife, May Whitty.

When I was on the stage, long before the First World War, I got my chance in a light comedy by H. V. Esmond called *Eliza Comes to Stay*. It was being tried out at Brighton, and the lady who played 'the other woman'— Eva Moore was the star—had been taken ill. I was given two days to get the part.

I can re-feel that suffocating sense of excitement as I learned my lines in the slow train jog-jogging down to Brighton, and the ordeal of rehearsing with my first star, dear Ben Webster. He didn't behave like my idea of a star. He seemed to know all about being scared silly and his blessed kindness and patience amazed me. But I have always found that the better an actor is the more patient he is likely to be with beginners. Actresses—no!

Ben Webster's special gift, apart from charm and good looks, was the one which Hamlet singles out for praise— smoothness. It must have been an inherited characteristic, for his grandfather, the first Ben Webster, was a controlling influence of the mid-Victorian stage world. He built the new Adelphi, ruled at the Haymarket and the St James's wrote his own plays, polished other people's and was a famous character-actor into the bargain.

My Ben Webster married May Whitty, who must have played as many parts as there are days in the year. She is perhaps best remembered for her performance in Emlyn Williams's *Night Must Fall*. It was put on at the Duchess, the little theatre built off Covent Garden some ten years after the end of the First World War, and Dame May played the old lady murdered by the young crook. It was an extraordinary performance. She never left her wheel-chair and she was meek, affectionate and terrified; but she dominated the stage and the play.

She dominated in real life also; for apart from her theatre-work she had a restless energy of goodness. Once—it was during the First World War—she discovered in a public asylum a pauper patient who had an obsession that she could not open her eyes. The place was badly under-staffed, and the case was considered hopeless, so she had lain month after month, washed and fed but otherwise ignored, till what had been an obsession became a physical fact: the eyelids were so inflamed that they were sealed to the cheeks. May Whitty found this out and, busy as she was with war-work, made time to go every day to sit with the poor creature, talk to her and bathe and poultice her eyes. One day, after many weeks, the eyes opened.

The Websters' only child, Margaret, must have a closer acquaintance with the Actors' Church than anyone in the world. She was born within the precincts: she was christ-ened in the font: her perambulator was put out into the churchyard before she could walk. In the early days when she was playing at the Old Vic—she was a very fine Lady Macbeth—her abiding ground was Covent Garden.

Later she went to New York to put on *Richard II* for Maurice Evans. A series of Shakespeare plays followed, and I believe she is the first woman to have produced opera at the Met. The capacity to direct, of course, she gets from Dame May; but it is a calmer and less impulsive talent. I once saw her cope with a dozen stars who were giving an unrehearsed one-day show at the barn in Tenterden in memory of Ellen Terry, and the show went without a hitch. She reminded me then of her father.

The Websters settled down in Hollywood in their old age, and their Spanish-type house instantly became the Bedford Street flat with St Paul's, Covent Garden in the background. There they both died. But after the war, when things had once more settled down, I happened to go into St Paul's one morning and the Rector, who had been an actor himself and took the keenest interest in all his parishioners, caught me on the way out.

'You are coming to the service tomorrow, aren't you?'

'I don't think I can, you know. I have to be at the studio.'

'But tomorrow Ben and May are coming home.'

IV

St Paul's, Covent Garden

St Paul's, Covent Garden, has as odd a history as any church in London.

To begin with, it was built for a congregation not yet in existence, as a grudged necessity if the land development was to go through. For some years it stayed unconsecrated; for the incumbent of St Martin's, the Reverend William Bray, didn't approve of a new parish at his back-door; but in 1638 it was at length established as a Chapel of Ease, and finally it became an independent church with its own Rector. Within a few years it was the rage, and everybody who was anybody had to be seen at morning service. Pepys often worshipped there. The victor of La Hogue paid ten pounds a year for his seat in the gallery. The Bishop of Armagh was preaching at this fashionable church when James II sent for him to come at once to the palace, and the Bishop sent back a saucy message—when he had ended his service to God he would make time for the King. An inverted snob, that Bishop of Armagh, or else a prophet who could tingle at the electricity in the air, and knew that the coming storm would wreck King James the Second.

But before the church had seen out its century there was a change in its fortunes. It did not 'draw' as well as it had done in Pepys's time, as a playful letter in *The Spectator* makes only too clear. It purports to come from the Sexton of St Paul's, who complains that the members of his congregation went to see Powell's puppet-show in the Piazza when they ought to have been in church. 'There now appear among us none but a few ordinary people, who come to church only to say their prayers. . . . I have placed my son at the Piazza to acquaint the ladies that the Bell rings for Church, and that it stands on the other side of the Garden; but they only laugh at the child.'

A fire occurred not long after the church was built. Repairs were at once put in hand, but the beautiful design was injured by the bad taste of the parishioners, who insisted on alterations. When the church was properly restored a little later they had to pay four thousand pounds for their fun. Then came a second fire and a second restoration; but by then St Paul's, Covent Garden, was no longer fashionable. It became the Actors' Church, the Market Church, and as London grew more crowded actors and market-men began to move out to the suburbs, and so the congregation continued to dwindle. The side-galleries 'hung with tapestries' were no longer needed and at last were taken down.

Today, however, St Paul's, Covent Garden, is once more a busy centre. There are services for healing the sick, services for blessing animals, musical Sundays, flower Sundays, birthday parties and a Christmas market. There are early morning services, and Communion is followed by a Parish Breakfast. The St Bartholomew massacre is commemorated: a sermon is preached—subject, Tolstoy's *War and Peace*. The church is as various in its activities as the Garden and its theatres, and so modern in its outlook that it has recently spent a whole fifty pounds on electrifying the clock which faces the churchyard. The clock which faces the Market stopped long ago; but when another fifty pounds has been saved that will also be set going again.

The Inigo Place gates into the churchyard are closed at night, and so are the gates of the two tunnel exits into Henrietta Street and King Street. It is sad to remember that these three paths were once formal entrances lined with trees—pretty paths to a pleasant country church. In the daytime, however, the paths are still in constant use. People are for ever popping out from one of the tunnels like rabbits who know their warren, and bolting in at the other, or swinging briskly down the main path to Bedford Street, and always in their comings and goings they walk over graves—graves of poets, painters, musicians, politicians, honest citizens, fine ladies, prostitutes, and at least one murderer.

The murderer was Robert Carr, a favourite of James I, who for a time all-but ruled England. His closest friend was a young poet called Sir Thomas Overbury, and the two were inseparable. One day, however, Carr fell in love with a sophisticated young woman who had been married against her will to the son of Elizabeth's Essex. She in turn fell in love with Carr and petitioned for a nullity decree in order to marry him.

But Overbury was desperately jealous of the Countess and did all he could to separate her from Carr—he is said to have known facts about her marriage that could have prevented a separation. But she was the cleverer: she contrived his disgrace and got him sent to the Tower. There he died a few days before the law freed her from young Essex.

She and Carr then married; but a year later the growing scandal came to a head, and the pair were formally accused of having arranged Overbury's murder by slow poison. The trial horrified the country, especially when it learned that the victim had suffered agonies before he died. All the conspirators were found guilty, and several accomplices were hanged; but the scandal was not lessened when the principals were pardoned by King James, Carr at once and his wife two years later. But things went ill with them afterwards. Their world shut its gates against them, and they ended by hating each other.

It is a true story; but it might just as easily have been the invention of a Jacobean dramatist, for all the necessary ingredients are there—over-life-size characters, a mad plot, a full-length portrait of an ambiguous victim, a murderess, and a criminal who could be pitied; for Carr is supposed to have been accessory after the fact only. He lived another twenty years, and is linked with the Garden because his only child married the Earl of Bedford who laid out the Square. He was one of the first to be buried in the new churchyard.

Sunchild or criminal, it's all one to the churchyard. A few years later the actor Edward Kynaston was buried there, as beautiful and famous as Carr was beautiful and infamous. He was the last of the actors brought up in the Shakespeare tradition of boys in women's parts, and he played Juliet to Betterton's Romeo. Later in life he played men's parts with equal success and authority.

There exists an interesting print of Kynaston in his youth. He has the full lips and rounded forehead of a Rubens portrait, and large, well-shaped eyes that must have been blue. It is a countenance which could be easily disguised as a woman's; but it does not suggest effeminacy. The expression is at once alluring and formidable.

'Went to see the Cockpitt play, the first that I have had time to see since my coming from sea. *The Loyal Subject,* where one Kinaston, a boy, acted the Duke's sister, but made the loveliest lady that ever I saw in my life.'

This is Samuel Pepys speaking. Later in the same year he went to Ben Jonson's play *The Silent Woman* and saw Kynaston again, and was again enthusiastic.

'Kinaston the boy had the good turn to appear in three shapes: first, as a poor woman in ordinary clothes, to please Morose; then in fine clothes, as a gallant; and in them was clearly the prettiest woman in the whole house: and lastly, as a man; and then likewise did appear the handsomest man in the house.'

But all the accounts of Kynaston are attractive. He stays alive at the other end of the telescope just as Betterton and Garrick do. Garrick, Betterton, Kynaston—if ever we get time-travel those are the three actors I'd walk back through the centuries to see.

Wycherley the dramatist is another Restoration figure

who belongs to the Garden; for he lived in Bow Street and was buried in the churchyard. There have been great out-cries made against the Restoration dramatists: loose—coarse—immoral, and so on; but for a reasonable assessment it is worth listening to Charles Lamb; for as a critic he was past-master of the lost art of putting his finger on what was worth while in a play—or a dramatist:

'In our anxiety that our morality should not take cold, we wrap it up in a great blanket surtout of precaution against the breeze and sunshine. . . . I do not know how it is with others, but I feel the better always for the perusal of one of Congreve's —nay, why should I not add even of Wycherley's—comedies. I am the gayer at least for it.'

For Wycherley's quality as a man the authority is Pope, who was a boy of sixteen when the dramatist was sixty-four; but in spite of that gap of years there was friendship and true attachment between them. Pope was not famous for lenity; but he was always tender with Wycherley. At twenty-one he is writing: 'The love of some things rewards itself, as of Virtue and of Mr Wycherley,' and later: 'He never did an unjust thing to me in his whole life.'

A much less important dramatist buried in the church-yard is of special interest to women. After Davenant opened the theatre-door to actresses, intelligent women, ever hopeful, began to write plays. No genius arose; but the first of the women dramatists, Afra Behn, was effective and entertaining, and her principal successor, Mrs Cent-livre, was something of a portent.

She had been an actress herself, and all her plays show what a working knowledge of the stage can do for a dramatist. It made her, for one thing, completely objective. The abuse of Mrs Behn is largely based on her obstinate femininity. She wrote no more coarsely than her contempor-aries; but she seems coarser because her women are realized as actual people, and what is a mere convention of obscenity in the mouth of a puppet becomes shocking when the puppet comes to life. But Susannah Centlivre never wrote anything which makes the reader say: 'Here is the purely feminine point of view,' or: 'This could only have been written by a woman.' She was not inspired; but she was immensely competent, coolly accepting and skilfully exploiting the conventions of a masculine theatre. She understood fun, and she had a pleasant sense of humour.

She had also an instinct for a good theatrical idea. In *A Bold Stroke for a Wife* the plot depends on the fact that a pretty girl is left in the charge of four guardians, a man-about-town, a canting hypocrite, a tradesman and an antiquary. If she marries without the signed consent of all four she loses her fortune. By variously disguising himself the lover, Feignwell, contrives to conciliate the first three guardians. The fourth backs another candidate, Simon Pure. So Feignwell ends by masquerading as Pure and manages to secure the last consent before the real Simon Pure turns up. It is all most adroitly managed.

But the play of hers which I like best is called *A Wonder: A Woman Keeps a Secret*, and my wonder is that, with the present rage for out-of-copyright revivals, no one has brought it back to some stage in-the-round; for it was popular for over a century. As late as 1829 Washington Irving writes from Dresden to the young American painter, C. R. Leslie, that he is involved in private theatricals at the house of an English lady. 'I . . . am on the point of playing Don Felix in *The Wonder*.'

To enjoy the play a modern audience has of course to concede two points. It must first accept the formal dialogue then fashionable. Then it will be able to enjoy hearing this repeatedly ruined by Mrs Centlivre's instinctive and unquenchable naturalness. Second, it must accept the convention that grown women could be forced into marriage or a nunnery by their guardians.

The Wonder was in Garrick's repertory for years, and he chose it for his farewell on 'this present Monday, June 10th 1776'. The flat statement of date is startling. It doesn't seem possible that Garrick retired from the theatre nearly two hundred years ago—not Garrick. Burbage belongs to the past—yes—and Betterton and even the Kembles, and certainly Kean. But Garrick in the oddest way is still of our time. He's an elder statesman, certainly; but one has the conviction that one might easily have seen him by luck, in youth, as one chanced to see some of the last actors of the last century—Wyndham and Dan Leno and Bernhardt.

Garrick's part in *The Wonder* was the hero Felix, and Kitty Clive used to play the heroine, Violante. They must have been wonderful together, the bickering, life-long friends, the two finest players of their day. When Kitty Clive retired she also chose *The Wonder* for her farewell performance, and Garrick played her lover in scenes that suited them both to perfection.

For *The Wonder* is Violante herself, a woman who keeps a friend's secret at the risk of her own happiness. The part of the lover, Felix, is even richer. In it Garrick could run through every mood in an actor's repertory—humour, suspicion, jealousy, tenderness, temper, reproachful fury—till in the last act he is provided with lines tender and sensitive enough to be moving even when read, and read in bad small print at that.

The lovers have been raging at each other. Felix, mad with jealousy of a certain Scotch Colonel, tells Violante that she has lost her reputation, and announces his final departure. She, as quick tempered as he, flames up, tells him that she doesn't care how soon he takes his leave, and turns her back on him. There is an uneasy pause, each unwilling to take the final step. At last Violante bursts into tears. It then begins to dawn on Felix that just possibly his suspicions are unfounded. He begins questioning her all over again, and this time every word she says makes him the more ashamed of himself.

Here is the end of that scene—and for the sake of a proper imagining, call the two players by their real names and remember that both are beloved by the audience that is saying goodbye to one of them. He is an aging man, smallish, with a brilliant eye, a quick-silver expression and a voice that can charm a bird off a bough. She, a born comedienne, is fifty but still irresistible. She sits crying: he stands at the door, between going and coming, watching her.

GARRICK: And do you not know this Scotch colonel?

KITTY CLIVE: Pray ask me no more questions. This night shall clear my reputation, and leave you without excuse for your base suspicions. More than this I shall not satisfy you; therefore, pray leave me.

GARRICK: Didst thou ever love me, Violante?

KITTY CLIVE: I'll answer nothing. You were in haste to be gone just now; I should be very well pleased to be alone, sir.

> [*She sits down and turns aside.*]

GARRICK: I shall not long interrupt your contemplation. [*aside*] Stubborn to the last!

KITTY CLIVE: [*aside*] Did ever woman involve herself as I have done?

GARRICK: [*aside*] Now would I give one of my eyes to be friends with her; for something whispers to my soul she is not guilty.

(*He pauses; then pulls up a chair and sits by her at a little distance, looking at her some time without speaking, then draws a little nearer to her.*)

GARRICK: Give me your hand at parting, however, Violante, won't you? (*He lays his hand upon her knee several times.*) Won't you—won't you—won't you?

KITTY CLIVE: (*half regarding him*) Won't I do what?

GARRICK: You know what I would have, Violante. Oh! My heart!

These two belonged to Covent Garden in life; but in death the Abbey claimed Garrick. He lies in Poets' Corner at the foot of Shakespeare's monument, and Kitty Clive's memory was preserved by the urn in Walpole's garden.

But it is remarkable how many theatre people—dramatists, actors, artists, musicians, craftsmen—have been

72

housed at last in the Market churchyard, though where they lie is no longer known. There exists a picture of it in 1820. The two raised lawns are packed with graves, each with an upright headstone. But the stones were taken down many years ago and used to pave the walks.

Even so it was a rather gloomy and forlorn God's acre when I first knew it. The two trees-of-heaven were dusty, the grass of the lawns looked tired, and flowers were only to be seen in late July when the catalpa-tree which marks an ancient plague-pit broke into its economical blossoming. The white panicles are handsomely streaked with tan and purple, but the single blooms are set farther apart than they are on the candlesticks of the generous horse-chestnut. As I watched my terrier careering over the dusty grass I used to long to start gardening.

But last autumn, after some years absence, I found a churchyard transformed. Flower-beds had been cut in the lawns, and these blazed with geraniums and dahlias. The grass was velvety, there was an arch of roses, and two urns on either side of the four steps leading up to the vestibule overflowed with colour. The little place had become as gay and charming a garden as you could find in London, and all the work had been done by two friends of the church, for love. The Londoner doesn't change. He must have his garden.

There were also many more seats than there used to be in the 'thirties, all spruced up with new paint—according to tradition. As early as 1656 the church-wardens paid to the painter for painting the benches and seats in the Market Place One Pound ten shillings. The churchyard seats are always occupied. There are the regular lunchers, the occasional lunchers, nurses from the nearby Charing Cross Hospital, young actors easing off between rehearsals at the Adelphi and the Vaudeville, and, of course, the market-men. Harry, the hall-porter at Boulestin's and everybody's friend, could generally be seen after the luncheon rush was over easing off on one of the benches with a book, and another regular client was a battered old man in clean, ragged clothes and a hat with half the crown gone, hair streaming over his shoulders and a long beard. He always carried a cut-down ponytrap-umbrella and a tied-up handkerchief full of crumbs for the sparrows. I once made a little sketch of him in bronze, which now sits in Long Acre in Val Gielgud's writing-room; for Val Gielgud is a Covent Garden man from the old Savoy Hill days when he was starting the B.B.C.'s Dramatic Department, and he knew and liked the old gentleman with the sparrows.

When I was back in the Garden churchyard a few weeks ago I missed the sparrow-man. Too many faces disappeared in that grey six years. But except for that gap the sprinkling of people on the seats looked exactly as they had always done, sitting as they always sat, faded people, looking at nothing in particular and resting as quietly as the dead who share the garden with them. They never look up when somebody comes briskly in from Inigo Place and strides past them into the church.

The church of St Paul's, Covent Garden, is unlike any other church. Every book ever written about the Garden re-tells Walpole's anecdote of the owner calling in Inigo Jones to plan the new square and telling him that there would have to be a church, but that he, the owner, did not want to spend too much. 'In short,' said he, 'I will not have it much better than a barn,' on which the architect promised him the handsomest barn in England.

People have argued ever since about that barn. Walpole did not admire the design. He said that the portico of the east front was a sham, and that anyway he didn't care much for the Tuscan order of architecture. But then there were so many things and people that Walpole didn't care much for.

He didn't care much for Dante:

'Dante was extravagant, absurd, disgusting, in short a Methodist parson in Bedlam.'

74

or Wesley:

'He is wondrous clean, but as evidently an actor as Garrick.'

or Mrs Siddons:

'What I really wanted, but did not find, was originality, which announces genius, and without both which I am never intrinsically pleased. All Mrs Siddons did, good sense or good instruction might give. I dare to say that were I one-and-twenty I should have thought her marvellous.'

He didn't care much for Garrick.

'Yes, Madam, I do think the pomp of Garrick's funeral perfectly ridiculous. It is confounding the immense space between pleasing talents and national service. . . . I do not at all mean to detract from Garrick's merit, who was a real genius in his way. Still, I cannot think that acting, however perfectly, what others have written is one of the most astonishing talents. . . . In declamation I confess he never charmed me; nor could he be a gentleman.'

Well—opinion is opinion; but Walpole's opinion should be weighed against Johnson's verdict, when Johnson was being badgered by Gibbon. This, according to Sir Joshua Reynolds, is what Gibbon said about Garrick and this is how the Doctor answered him.

GIBBON: I have been told . . . that Garrick, in company, had not the easy manners of a gentleman.

JOHNSON: Sir, I don't know what you may have been told, or what your ideas may be of the manners of a gentleman; Garrick had no vulgarity in his manners; it is true Garrick had not the airiness of a fop, nor did he assume an affected indifference to what was passing; he did not lounge from the table to the window, or from thence to the fire, or, whilst you were addressing your discourse to him, turn from you and talk to his next neighbour, or give any indication that he was tired of his company; if such manners form your idea of a fine gentleman, Garrick certainly had them not.

So you pay your money and you take your choice, always remembering that Walpole most definitely didn't care for Johnson's opinion either. 'The saucy Caliban! I don't know when I shall get you his blubber.'

But how can the borzoi consort with the bulldog?

As to the portico of St Paul's, Walpole had settled himself in a miniature neo-Gothic castle uglier than the worst Victorian Gothic, so it is clear that he could not possibly feel cosy with the Tuscan order. But he owns that the 'sham' was no fault of Inigo Jones. The design for the lovely square—and to judge by early prints Covent Garden was once the loveliest square in London—required that the church should command the Garden from the west, and the architect had arranged therefore that his portico should face east. It was a splendid one, with columns which Gay admired for their plain magnificence. The effect was dignified, not too big for its purpose, pleasing to the eye. The portico should have been the main entrance.

Unfortunately both patron and architect had forgotten that an altar must always be placed at the east end of a church. Inigo Jones had designed his masterpiece sacerdotally speaking, the wrong way round.

In a conflict between artistic rightness and religious decorum religion is bound to win, which is why the splendid portico became a sham. The portico has been used ever since as a way of escape from the crowded pavements and as a platform for speakers at elections. In Hogarth's time there was a coffee-house type of tavern squeezed up against it. During the last war it was once more a shelter for a coffee-stall.

Seen from the west, however, it is plain enough that Inigo Jones had kept his promise, and that, much as he admired a classical frontage, he had also looked lovingly at English barns. His side-walls are built of rose-brown brick. His windows are big and simple. The shallow slopes of the roof brood protectively over the walls. The Inigo vocabulary of brick and stone is here used to explain that town and country can meet, and that each needs the other.

The main path is paved with tombstones. The inscriptions are now too worn to read; but one is recorded in Stow which is surprising. It runs:

> 'Good Friend for Jesus Sake forebear
> To dig the Dust enclosed here.
> Blest be the Man that spares these Stones,
> And cursed be he that moves my Bones.'

But that is the Shakespeare inscription at Stratford! Exactly! So what is it doing in the year seventeen hundred in Covent Garden? Did some passionate admirer of Shakespeare insist on an identical inscription?

It is more likely that it was a commonplace, popular verse for use on gravestones, much as Blenheim and The Cedars were popular names for semi-detached suburban houses in the Edwardian age. But in one dead-against-Shakespeare volume those verses were quoted as the sort of thing a Stratford butcher's boy *would* write! I should like to make the author look up Stow—the Strype continuation, Book VI, Chapter VI. That would cool him.

But there is another inscription quoted on the same page that cools me.

> 'Oh Passer-by,
> Thou, thou must die
> As well as I.
> My soul's at rest,
> But thine's opprest;
> My State is best.
> Then let thy Care and Pleasure be
> To serve thy God and rest with me.'

Wonderfully easing to encounter that little verse, suddenly, amid the irritations of daily life.

To the left of the west front lies Samuel Butler, buried

77

six feet deep with his feet touching the church wall. This is not the Samuel Butler who wrote *Erewhon*, nor his grandfather, the Samuel Butler who was headmaster of Shrewsbury and once, quaintly, triumphed over Coleridge with a prize poem. It is the first Samuel Butler who lies here, the author of *Hudibras*, a satire on the seventeenth-century Puritans.

> Such as do build their faith upon
> The holy text of pike and gun. . . .
> Call fire, and sword, and desolation,
> A godly thorough reformation. . . .
> As if religion were intended
> For nothing else but to be mended.
> A sect whose chief devotion lies
> In odd perverse antipathies. . . .
> Compound for sins they are inclin'd to
> By damning those they have no mind to:
> Still so perverse and opposite,
> As if they worshipp'd God for spite.'

England and London were recovering from twenty years of this sort of thing when *Hudibras* was published, and the ludicrous adventures of a Roundhead Don Quixote naturally delighted the returning Royalists. In an age of wit it was accounted the wittiest satire in the language, and King Charles carried a copy in his pocket.

Only one man of brains and intelligence disagreed— Samuel Pepys. His distressful account of how he tried in vain to enjoy *Hudibras* is as amusing as *Hudibras* itself.

He begins by telling us how he went to his bookseller's and there picked up 'a new book of drollery in use, called "Hudibras" . . . cost me 2s. 6d. But when I come to read it, it is so silly an abuse of the Presbyter Knight going to the wars, that I am ashamed of it; and by and by meeting at Mr Townsend's at dinner, I sold it to him for 18d.'

That was in 1662, the day after Christmas. Boxing Day was not an Act of Parliament holiday in those days, and so the shops were open. But everybody was rocking with laughter over *Hudibras,* and Pepys hated to be out of the fashion, so in February he was trying again.

'I walked up and down and looked upon the outside of the new theatre building in Covent Garden, which will be very fine, and so to a bookseller's in the Strand, and there bought "Hudibras" again, it being certainly some ill-humour to be so against that which all the world cries up to be the example of wit; for which I am resolved once more to read him, and see whether I find I can like it or no.'

He didn't like it.

By the end of November the second part of *Hudibras* has appeared and Pepys is unhappier than ever:

'Looked upon the second part of "Hudibras" which I buy not but borrow to read, to see if it be as good as the first which the world cried up almightily, though it hath not a good liking in me, though I had tried by twice or three times reading to bring myself to think it witty.'

For the next ten days Pepys seems to have struggled manfully with the second volume; but it was not in him to enjoy Samuel Butler; so he settles for the best of both worlds. His library shall be fashionable, but his diary shall be honest. He goes to his bookseller's and, after leafing through Chaucer, Stow, Shakespeare, Jonson and others, he at last buys Fuller's *Worthies,* some Letters of State and —resentfully—'*Hudibras,* both parts, the book now in greatest fashion for drollery, though I cannot, I confess, see enough where the wit lies.' As the author of *Hudibras* would say, and indeed *did* say:

> 'He that complies against his will
> Is of his own opinion still.'

Butler is reputed to have died in want, though not in debt. I read somewhere that he was a red-head and had the temperament which goes with it, bitterly resenting neglect

and yet refusing to seek recognition. He was buried in the
Garden churchyard with a little group of twenty people
to say goodbye to him, his old friend Aubrey among them.
A tablet was put up to him in the church, and later a
monument was erected to his memory in the Abbey, which
made everyone feel comfortable till Wesley, the 'wondrous
clean man' of Walpole's sneer, ruined the general complacency by his bitter comment.

> 'The Poet's fate is here in emblem shown.
> He asked for bread, and he received a stone.'

To enter the church you go up some shallow steps past
Butler's unmarked resting-place and pass through a narrow
vestibule into the nave, which again has the look of a
splendid urbanized barn. This must be far more noticeable
today with the side-galleries gone than it was when St
Paul's, Covent Garden was first built. Turner's pencil
sketch of the interior hangs in the vestry and gives a hint
of what it all once looked like. Today, looking up, one feels
that something important is missing. These squarish
seventeenth-century churches need the relief of light-
caught upper rows of faces and a lively ceiling, and fire
long ago destroyed the ceiling paintings. But the lack of
colour is felt only when the church is full. Empty, the
effect is curiously soothing, with the noise from the Market
and the two streets quite shut off. The quiet is as gentle as
dust, and the emptiness has a vague, faint scent of dried
herbs, especially in autumn. Herbs, by the way, once had a
recognized place in the church; for an early herb-merchant
surprisingly got leave from the Rector of his day to store
all his merchandise in the church loft; but he had great
trouble in getting his sweet-smelling bundles moved in and
out.

Some say that Claude Duval, quiet at last, lies under the
paved central way to the altar, and what does he care that
Butler, lying beyond the wall, once made fun of him?
Others are sure that his body was later stolen away. A

third party indignantly denies that St Paul's ever harboured him. A highwayman buried in a church? Unthinkable! People grow quite violent about the matter—after two and a half centuries.

Charles Macklin, whose body lies far down beneath the altar, was another turbulent adventurer. He was an Irishman, and he cut a figure in the theatre-life of his day, which was also Garrick's day. He wrote a couple of successful plays, was a good actor and a great Shylock: the first player to treat the character as a tragic one. But his behind-scenes life was all turbulence. He actually killed a colleague in some petty greenroom fuss about a wig—this was at Drury Lane—stabbing him in the eye with a stage-dagger. He was tried for the killing and was lucky to be acquitted. This adventure was recorded in the memorial in the church. The inscription is crowned by the mask of theatrical convention; but—a comment on the taste of the age—the mask has a dagger through the eye.

The horrible misadventure did not cure Macklin. Garrick was his closest friend, but he quarrelled with him and did his best to ruin him. He quarrelled with his managements. He quarrelled with his audiences. Very often he won his battles. His memorial tablet claims that he fought death for a hundred and seven years, though the Encyclopaedia disputes with him over the last ten. Anyway death had the better of Macklin's last quarrel.

A hundred and seven years—how elastic time is! It stretches out—out—then it crumples suddenly into nothing, like a boy's catapult, easily pocketed. My grandfather, whom I knew pretty well, was ninety-seven when he died, and his father was fifty when he was born. So in 1963 someone lives who has talked to someone who knew someone who saw the performance of an actor born in the reign of Queen Anne.

Today St Paul's is still the Actors' Church, and yearly more names are added to the church's records and memories. Fred Terry, Denis Neilson-Terry, Charles Cochran,

Ivor Novello, Leslie Henson, MacQueen Pope, Bransby Williams—the century is growing old too quickly.

Far up on the right wall is a casket holding the ashes of Ellen Terry.

St Paul's, Covent Garden, is always open and never quite empty; though out of service hours there are seldom more than three people in it at a time. Somebody slips in quietly, makes for a pew, kneels a moment, then sits back and is still, and after five minutes slips quietly out again. You never see a verger, though the place is beautifully kept. The shape of Grinling Gibbons's pulpit soothes the eyes. The organ is being played: the sound is soft, rich and thrilling, yet held in check: it accompanies the quiet, it does not break in upon it. A pew in St Paul's, Covent Garden, is a wonderful place to make-over one's mind.

During the war I got to know its anxious guardian, Vincent Howson, a cheerful, energetic, sick man, passionately concerned for the needs of his parish. A porter once told me that in the first days 'parson' had gone round the Market and got hold of the name and regiment of every man who had joined-up, and from then on St Paul's sent monthly good wishes and cigarettes till the bad times were over. We made friends because of the Rector's other passionate interest, the theatre—he once carried a spear at Stratford—and I learned to respect his tireless devotion to his work, and warmed to his quaint kindliness.

The old church acquired a new look in his day. Its outer side-walls were cleaned, the interior began to smell of polish as well as herbs, and he was particularly proud of the tidy churchyard and the scrubbed steps of the western entrance. He couldn't bear sandwich papers, and was always putting up notices against bringing dogs into the churchyard. But though I have often seen him eye some small beast kicking up its heels on the forbidden grass and turn to frown dramatically upon the furtive owner, he never quite brought himself to shoo them out. He had a gift for making casual visitors feel that the church wanted them to come in, and arranged special service hours to suit the needs of the Market's shifting population. He was once a curate under Prebendary Clarence May, the present Rector, and it is pleasant to know that the old church is now in the care of the man who trained him. I realized what the training had been when a newspaper reported that all the Punch-and-Judy men of England had met the day before at St Paul's, Covent Garden, to celebrate the three hundredth anniversary of Mr Punch's first performance in England. One of the Toby-dogs had barked in church; but he was not turned out.

Coming or going you will almost certainly encounter a brisk lady—she is getting on for eighty-six—who is the encyclopaedia of St Paul's, Covent Garden. She can tell you with equal instantaneity where the prayerbooks are kept and where the great dead lie; for she has devoted the best part of her life to the needs of the Market church. She might be Oswy, that Saxon lady who lived by the shrine of King Edmund, and to the day of her death saw to it that the martyred saint had everything neat and handsome about him.

Her modern name is Miss Pitt, and her vestry is on the right going in; but if she sees that visitors are interested she will sometimes take them across to the Vicar's vestry on the left and show them a fine clock, made when mahogany was first brought to England—King Street, Covent Garden, was famous for its workers in mahogany. Nobody knows when the clock was made; but a bill for repairs is carefully preserved—the date 1795. All the church records are kept in the Rector's Vestry. The visitor carries away time-juggling impressions of fine parchments, finer handwriting, records of the Great Plague, five-shilling fines for swearing, and the story of the man who got off with a half-fine because he looked after an orphan who would otherwise have been a charge on the parish, a Nativity play directed in 1927 by Ellen Terry's daughter, Edith Craig, and an entry stating that one of the churchwardens had

83

paid his fee of three guineas for a pew-rent. The church-warden was David Garrick Esq.

There is also an inscription over the vestry-door which begins: 'Praise God for Henry Mosse, Rector of this church, who was killed in an air-raid in the early morning of the 29th January A.D. 1918 while ministering to his people.' A recent addition to the collection is the photograph of the Memorial Service to a fireman killed in the fire beneath the Covered Way in 1949.

I remember that fire. Under the Market are endless rabbit-runs, and there the Christmas hollies and laurels are dipped in buckets of gold and silver paint. This is inflammable stuff, and on that unlucky winter day a bucket caught fire. The Covered Way was exactly opposite my window, and I did a painting of the smoke curling up from under the edge of the pavement opposite, and the red fire-engines, and the two policemen keeping back the watching crowd. Nobody knew at the time that anyone had been killed. All such records Miss Pitt can show you. You scuff your way through the centuries as if you were walking in an autumn wood through dead leaves.

North of the churchyard lies King Street, as famous as Henrietta Street for its yesterdays.

A mansion stands at the north-west end of the Market. The Piazza joins it, clings to it, as if knowing that while that famous house stands there is safety for brick and stone. Today the beautiful place is occupied by one of the great Market firms, the doorway has been yanked out, and the ground-floor is given over to wholesale display. But once it was the finest house in the North Piazza, which in itself was one of the most important social centres in London.

An early occupant was that creature of fantasy, Sir Kenelm Digby. There is only one word with which to describe his career, and that is the very horrid one—'colourful'. He began life as an infant prodigy. At seventeen he was boasting of a love-affair with an aging Queen of France.

He was a brilliantly successful Naval Commander. He was in Spain with the future Charles I when the Prince was unsuccessfully wooing the Infanta, which was lucky for Digby; for the Prince married Henrietta Maria of France, and in later years Digby became her 'chancellor'. He made a romantic secret marriage with Venetia Stanley, who was reputed to be the most beautiful and brilliant woman of her time, and when she died he mourned her with passionate extravagance.

But it was not the end of life for him. Eight years later he was in Paris fighting a duel with a Frenchman who insulted Charles I, and he killed his man. Soon after he was imprisoned by the Roundhead Parliament. He was great for a time at Charles II's Court. When he fell from grace he settled down in Covent Garden as a man of letters and a dabbler in chemistry. By all accounts he was a handsome man with immense charm, a brilliant talker and—a romancer. Evelyn, who knew him well, occasionally mentions him in the Diary, but always as if he were lifting an eyebrow. 'He advised me to try and digest a little better, and gave me a water which he said was only rainwater of the autumnal equinox extremely rectified, very volatile. . . . But the truth is Sir Kenelm was an arrant mountebank.' And again, speaking of a lady with an allergy: 'Sir Kenelm tells us that laying but a rose upon her cheek it raised a blister; but Sir Kenelm was a teller of strange things.'

Some years later Admiral Russell took over the beautiful house and garden—'Digby's garden'. Russell was the grandson of the Earl of Bedford who built the Square, and is remembered as the man who beat the French at La Hogue in 1792. He is said to have used wood from his victorious but crippled flagship the *Britannia* to rebuild his staircase.

He was followed by Lord Archer, who also did much to beautify the house; but his occupancy had ill-effects on the façade of the church. It always seemed a shame that the steps of the portico should have been reduced; for the absence of approach dwarfs the frontage. The other day I came across a Victorian book of anecdotes which disclosed what had happened.

Lord Archer had a father-in-law, a Mr West, an M.P., very rich and important. He was also elderly, and as time went by he found the pavement levels awkward when he got out of his carriage. On hearing this the Covent Garden surveyor of pavements and his superior agreed together to raise the level of the Market pavement by three feet. Mr West was then able to get in and out of his carriage without being bothered by steps. The names of the vandals concerned were Mr Margund and Mr Grognon. I couldn't wish them uglier names.

Later the house became a hostelry and went downhill. It was rescued from a slum finish by Evans, an enterprising actor from Covent Garden, who made it famous for nearly a hundred years as Evans's Grand Hotel, Music and Supper Rooms. I possess an adorable pamphlet issued by the management giving the hotel's history as well as information on a bewildering variety of subjects—Covent Garden dramatists, performing fleas, the Chester mysteries, Gellert, Gregory the Great, hymnology in France, lists of former inhabitants of Covent Garden, a print of a quack doctor, Covent Garden authors, Covent Garden painters, a description of a new sweating-house called The Hummums— still surviving when P. G. Wodehouse was writing his first pieces—letters from Weber, notes on barley broth, the full story of how Grinling Gibbons's house in Bow Street collapsed, and a pathetic complaint published in a newspaper called *The Compleat Tradesman* against the setting up of shops in 'the portigoo', as Cockneys used to call the Piazza, on the ground that it was ruining the City's trade. 'There are some trades whose commodities are such that it would be very little more trouble for anybody to go into the City to buy them than to go to Covent Garden, such as woollen or linen cloth, or the like.' The article reads like a discussion on the Common Market.

It is difficult to believe that any hotel-keeper ever genuinely felt that such a compilation would interest his customers, and fascinating to realise that he was right. The book also gives the programmes at some of the musical evenings as well as copies of the words, and so we learn exactly what gentlemen in the first half of the nineteenth century enjoyed hearing after supper. The name of Sir Henry Bishop, the musical director at the Covent Garden Theatre, frequently occurs: his glee *The Chough and the Crow* was particularly popular. *The Miller's Daughter* by Tennyson was arranged for several voices, and *Live Henri Quatre!*, with a solo for a soprano, occurs in nearly all the programmes. The solo begins:

> 'Henri, adieu, my king, farewell,
> Do not forget your Gabrielle.'

It is even more difficult to believe that the London man-about-town in mad search of dissipation could settle down evening after evening in Evans's Music Rooms to listen to a song about rain called *Patter, patter, let it pour!*; but the programmes prove that it was so. The evenings became so popular that a little gallery was run up at the back so that ladies might attend. It was built out over 'Digby's Garden' where, in the years between, the Kembles had a cottage.

Coleridge lived for three years in King Street, earning his living as a journalist. It must have been hard for him—but harder for his editor. In one of Kipling's early stories this sentence occurs: 'Remember that in all the millions permitted there are no more than five—five little lines—of which one can say: "These are the pure Magic. These are the clear Vision. The rest is only poetry." ' And he adds that three of those five lines are to be found in Coleridge's *Kubla Khan*. So you see why I feel sympathetic towards that long-forgotten editor of a fashionable morning paper.

There is no trace of Coleridge in the Evans programmes, which is not surprising. But Dibdin of the thousand ballads also lived in King Street, and that no song of his reached the Music Room is very surprising indeed; for his work was once enormously popular. Even today everybody still knows *Tom Bowling*, though you don't hear *Saturday Night at Sea* as often as you did in the 'nineties. It's a pity, for the tune is as sweet as honeysuckle, and the two opening lines are magical.

> 'The moon on the ocean was dimmed by a ripple
> Affording a chequered delight.'

But the glory of King Street was a house which once stood on the south side. It was known as 'The Two Crowns and Cushions', and was occupied by an upholsterer called Arne. It was celebrated in Queen Anne's day because four Indian chiefs once stayed there for a whole fortnight. They had come from Canada on a mission to Queen Anne, their names sounded like a Chinese crossword puzzle, and they were as popular with the British public as four film-stars all living together would be today. 'I often mixed with the rabble,' murmurs Addison, blandly inventing, 'and followed them a whole day together.'

To entertain the Four Kings, as people called them, must have gratified every fibre of Mr Arne the upholsterer's being; for he is described as a noted busybody, much more interested in the King of Poland's affairs than in the doings of his neighbours. Indeed there is not much more to be said about Mr Arne, and his house was burnt down long ago. But—he had a son. The son used to practise the spinet at midnight, the strings muffled with a handkerchief for fear of being heard by his fusspot father. But if there is one tune which everybody in England knows it is the tune which that schoolboy was to write a few years later to Thomson's words. The first phrase is transcribed on his memorial plaque.

88

In   Memory of

THOMAS ARNE

Musician and Parishioner

1710—1778

Baptized in this Church

Buried in this Churchyard

+

Rule Britannia

Let us praise famous men . . . such as
found out musical tunes.

Ecclus. XLIV 1. 5.

V

Operatic

'After the meal he was taken to an enchanting spectacle. . .
composed of agreeable verses, delightful songs, dances that
expressed the soul's emotions and scenes that charmed the
eyes in discerning them. This form of pleasure which
brought together so many other forms was known only
by a foreign name; it was called opera.'

Voltaire.

The Princess of Babylon.

Opera! Opera! At the beginning of the seventeenth century
it was a novel word in theatre dressing-rooms. It came from
Italy, and news of sung dialogues and gorgeous sceneries
were reaching an England already in love with Court
masques.

Characteristically Shakespeare was one of the first to
explore the new art-form. From the moment in *The
Tempest* when Alonso exclaims: 'What harmony is this?'
and Gonzalo answers: 'Marvellous sweet music!' we are in
a different dimension of theatre. The illusions of the
banquet-scene—Ariel's trick appearance and speech before
he vanishes amid thunder-claps—is operatic. Again in
Act IV Shakespeare, or Prospero—which ever you call him
—once more interrupts the flow of the play proper with the
thin excuse that the betrothal of Ferdinand and Miranda
must be celebrated.

'Now come, my Ariel, bring a corollary
Rather than want a spirit: appear, and pertly!'

With that he joyously returns to his new game, playing

90

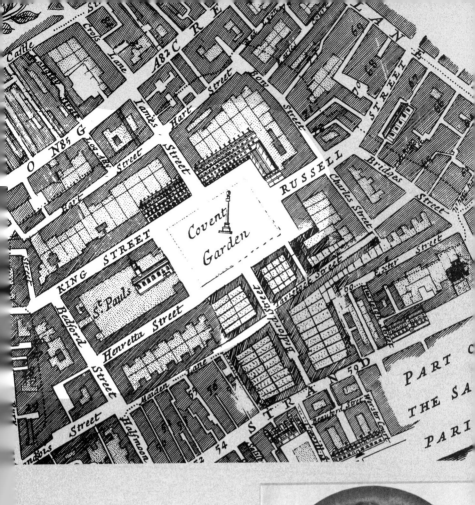

Carolean

with the operatic idea like a tiger playing with its cub, touching it lightly, backing from it in amusement, nosing it, patting it, shoving it about, teaching it to move and live, till at last, abandoning mere play, the huge, lithe mind-animal moves in one spring to the purely operatic climax of Juno's entrance, the song of blessing and the ballet.

'Enter certain reapers, properly habited: they join with the nymphs in a graceful dance; towards the end whereof Prospero starts suddenly, and speaks; after which, to a strange, hollow and confused noise, they heavily vanish.'

The operatic revels are now ended, and the playwright returns to his play and ends that also. If that conclusion includes his personal farewell to his art, it may be that he also intended it to be the farewell of spoken drama to undivided rule on the English stage.

But it was not till the Civil War was over that the form established itself in England. Till then, anyone genuinely interested in opera went, like John Evelyn, to Rome or Venice for it.

Evelyn was a Covent Garden man when he was in London. He had a brother living in Russell Street, and years later took lodgings for his family near by. But his home was in the country, and the family estates were situated in the Parliamentary zone. To have remained there when the Civil War broke would have ruined him 'without any advantage to his majesty,' as he is careful to point out; so he obtained a licence from the King to leave England. He headed for Italy.

To travel in a former Italy with Evelyn is better even than to travel in a former Italy with Goethe. The Renaissance summer was not yet over, the blooming was still prodigious, and at twenty-four Evelyn was a sort of human bee, antennae quivering for honey. Even before he landed he was writing of the 'peculiar joys of Italy—perfumes of orange, citron and jasmine flowers' carried to his ship on the shore-breeze. He lived through the next two years in a

91

state of quivering, sensuous delight that has no parallel till Keats came to earth.

He liked what e'er he looked on. He marvels at the *Last Judgement* in the Pope's Chapel 'by M. Angelo Buonarroti, of vast design and miraculous fancy'; but the orange-tree with a rose grafted on it is also a marvel. Nor does he forget to relate—you can hear the prim, embarrassed cough of the future moralist—that the courtesans of Naples slung eggs of sweet water into his coach during the Carnival.

'Indeed the town is so pestered with these cattle that there needs no small fortification to preserve from their enchantment while they display all their natural and artificial beauty, play, sing, feign compliment, and by a thousand studied devices seek to inveigle foolish young men.'

Evelyn had no intention of being a foolish young man; but a sigh hangs in the air. He was only twenty-four.

His ear was as acute as his eye. On an Italian first of March he was noting that 'it was a sweet morning and the bushes were full of nightingales'. He was careful to record the sounds of Holy Week, the firing of the great guns of the Castle of St Angelo, the dismal singing on Good Friday, the silence on the Saturday before Easter and the music on Easter Monday in the Chiesa Nuova. The climax of enjoyment, however, was a magnificent opera performed in the presence of the Pope's nephew, the governors of Rome, cardinals, ambassador and ladies.

In Ascension week of the same year, when he was staying in Venice, he went again to what had become 'the opera'. 'Comedies and other plays were represented in recitative music by the most excellent musicians, vocal and instrumental, with variety of scenes painted and contrived with no less art of perspective, and machines for flying in the air, and other wonderful notions; taken together, it is one of the most magnificent and expensive diversions the wit of man can invent. The history was Hercules in Lydia; the scenes changed thirteen times. . . . This held us by the eyes and ears till two in the morning,' after which he went on to see a gambling masquerade. The energy of twenty-four!

He even organized a voyage to the Holy Land; but the plan fell through—'after I had provided all necessaries, laid in snow to cool our drinks, bought some sheep, poultry, biscuit, spirits, and a little cabinet of drugs in case of sickness.' Now how did he get hold of snow in Venice, in June, and a June exceeding hot? He says he drank so much iced wine that he got a sore throat which nearly killed him.

It is curious that such a fierce capacity for enjoying the shows of life should have been so soon extinguished. Only ten years later, when he was staying in Covent Garden, Evelyn again saw an opera 'after the Italian way' but with an English libretto; but the experience was no longer a thrill. He found the piece 'much inferior to the Italian composure and magnificence,' and adds severely: 'It was prodigious that in a time of such public consternation such a vanity should be kept up or permitted.' But then, rather touchingly, he weakens. 'However, I being engaged with company, could not decently resist the going to see it, though my heart smote me for it.' The eggs of sweet water were not entirely forgotten.

But Evelyn's visit to opera in London at least proves that Shakespeare's experiment in *The Tempest* was at last showing dividends. Opera had arrived, and was settling in. The end-result, of course, was to be the Royal Opera House, Covent Garden. The connection is as tenuous as a spider's thread, but it exists, and can be followed back across Time's blackberry-bushes to the central Shakespearean web—thus:

There was a wealthy vintner living in Oxford in Shakespeare's day, and his wife, according to Aubrey, was 'a very beautiful woman of a very good wit and of conversation extremely agreeable'—as we should say, a charmer. Shakespeare used to stay with the Davenants at their hostelry on his journeys between Stratford and London, and he was godfather to the Davenants' son William.

93

People gossiped about the friendship between Shakespeare and Mrs Davenant. Pope told a story of how young Will Davenant came tearing home from school one day and was stopped by a don, who asked whither he was going in such haste. The boy said: 'To my godfather, Shakespeare.' 'Fie, child,' says the old gentleman, 'have you not learned yet that you should not use the name of God in vain?'

Modern critics pooh-pooh the rumour; but Aubrey, who knew Davenant well, says that when pleasant over a glass of wine with his intimate friends, Sir William would himself tell the story of his mother and Shakespeare, and 'seemed contented enough to be thought his son'.

At any rate the wistful verses which he wrote when, it is said, he was still a youngster, show that his godfather had captured his heart and his imagination. The lines suggest also that he had known Stratford in his godfather's lifetime, and visiting it later, or even for that April funeral in 1616, he had found the place—emptied.

> 'Beware, delighted poets, when you sing
>   To welcome nature in the early spring:
>   Your num'rous feet not tread
>   The banks of Avon; for each flower,
>   As it ne'er knew a sun or shower,
>   Hangs there the pensive head.
>
> The piteous river wept itself away
> Long since, alas, to such a swift decay,
>   That reach the map, and look
>   If you a river there can spie:
>   And for a river your mock'd eye
>   Will find a shallow brook.'

Davenant got his social training according to the custom of the day in a nobleman's house. Later he drifted to the theatre, wrote plays, worked on masques with Inigo Jones after the architect had split with Ben Jonson over billing procedure, and when Jonson died succeeded him as Poet Laureate. By 1639 he was managing the Phoenix

Theatre, which had replaced the Cockpit and was in turn
to be replaced by the Theatre Royal Drury Lane, and so
became a Covent Garden man.

The Civil War put an end to the venture; for, as
Davenant saw it, the Puritan 'was so offended with recreation as if he would accuse even nature herself to want
gravity for bringing in the spring so merrily with the
music of birds,' and the new government at once closed
down all theatres.

Many professionals were ruined; but there was a lot
of the Elizabethan in Davenant's composition, and disaster
appears to have stimulated him. He turned himself into
a sort of Scarlet Pimpernel 'for the duration', plotted and
counter-plotted, became a lieutenant-general, was knighted
for bravery by commission of Charles I, failed rather conspicuously as a diplomat, and thereafter had almost as many
improbable adventures as Sir Percy himself.

He was finally sent to the Tower, charged with high-
treason, and was in danger of trial and execution till, of all
people, Milton intervened to save him. The two were
friends in spite of their politics, and after the Restoration
Davenant in turn protected the greater man.

In the first years of his exile he began to write an inter-
minable heroic poem—indeed he never terminated it
—called *Gondibert* which was admired in its day. Pope
himself said of it: 'It was not a good poem if you take it in
the whole, but there are a great many good things in it.'
But today *Gondibert* is a Red Queen's biscuit—it does not
quench our thirst.

Yet it is worth dipping into for there is interesting stuff
in it and the wisdom that comes from fascinated, un-
romantical observation of life, brightened constantly by
typical Davenant flashes, playful and charming.

> ' "If sir," said he, "we heedlessly pass by
>   Great towns, like birds that from the country come
> But to be scared and on to forests fly;
>   Let's be no travelled fools, but roost at home!'

95

It's odd, but whenever Davenant writes of birds he takes on their qualities and becomes alert, airborne and musical.

Davenant published *Gondibert* as soon as he was out of the Tower, and then turned once more to his playwriting. Cromwell was still in control; but reaction against austerity had already begun, and when Davenant opened a small, private theatre in the City nobody interfered with him. There he produced the first opera with an English book, *The Siege of Rhodes.*

He had hit on the right moment. The war-weary sixteen-fifties had much the same attitude to the Elizabethan past as the nineteen-fifties to the Victorian past. 'I saw Hamlet played,' Evelyn wrote soon after the Restoration, 'but now the old plays begin to disgust this refined age.'

Davenant, always lively and up to the moment, grasped at once that here was the tired-businessman situation. The public didn't want to be made to think, and had no intention of using its imagination for years and years to come. At the same time it very much wanted to be amused. So Sir William proceeded to amuse it in the always best and easiest way, by giving it something new or something that the public thought of as new. His novelty was opera as the seventeenth century understood the term, with music, singing, a variety of sets and, best of all, an actress instead of a boy in the part of the heroine. Ianthe was first played by a Mrs Coleman; but it soon became Mrs Betterton's great part, and people referred to her as 'Ianthe' just as they talked of Butler as 'Hudibras'.

Ianthe is a plum of a part. She is noble, pure, beautiful. She sells her jewels and then is captured by the Emperor Solyman's forces as she is bringing the money to her husband Alonzo and the citizens of besieged Rhodes. Solyman falls madly in love with her; but in the best sentimental-heroic tradition lets her pass to her husband unharmed.

Alonzo, however, is a realist. He doesn't believe in Solyman's chivalry. Solyman's Empress doesn't believe in it either. So when the citizens of Rhodes insist that the popular Ianthe shall return to the Emperor to beg for peace a very pretty Monna Vanna situation is created, with fine opportunities for scenes of jealousy and anguish, as well as for magnificent dresses and sets, before the demanded happy ending.

The recipe is familiar, though the flavour is out of fashion. If the libretto is still rather charming reading it is because Davenant's warm, boyish, tingling personality pervades everything he writes. He can be very good and he can be extremely bad; but good or bad he is at least always living the story with his characters. His soldiers of all nations are convincing because he has known such soldiers in the wars. The sentiments of his women's chorus are lively and unexpected because the women he knew in his own life struck him as lively and unexpected, and his most conventional dialogue gives off sparks of poetry because he truly believed that 'poetry is the subtle engine by which the wonderful body of the opera must move.' Even when he confused poetry with heroics his instinct could often be trusted to save him. The chorus of wives singing about jealousy is an example of how his natural humour is always breaking down the conventions which he believed himself to respect.

FIRST WIFE: This cursed jealousy, what is't?
SECOND WIFE: 'Tis love that has lost itself in a mist.
THIRD WIFE: 'Tis love being frighted out of his wits.
FOURTH WIFE: 'Tis love that has a fever got;
                Love that is violently hot;
                But troubled with cold and trembling fits.
                'Tis yet a more unnatural evil:
CHORUS: 'Tis the god of love, 'tis the god of love, possessed
                with a devil.

After the Restoration Shakespeare's godson had his headquarters in Lincoln's Inn Fields, and until his death, half a century after a certain unforgotten April funeral, his

D

career continued to be brilliant. There is only one big black blot on it—his 'improvements' of Shakespeare's plays.

It is obvious that Sir William was distressed that his godfather's plays were going out of fashion; but, like all extroverts, he couldn't be content to shrug and pity the fools: he had to be constructive. Unfortunately his training in masque and opera hampered him exactly as too many years in Hollywood hamper modern playwrights and directors. Also he had at his elbow Dryden, and Dryden, though he could achieve his own *Antony and Cleopatra*, was not a born dramatist. His genius walked in other paths. He was a great poet and knew, perhaps, that Shakespeare was a greater one—he says somewhere that Davenant had first taught him to venerate Shakespeare—and he agreed with the troubled godson that something must be done.

'Yes, you may tag my verses,' Milton said when Dryden asked his leave to turn *Paradise Lost* into a rhymed drama; which is as if the Recording Angel should say to one of the Major Prophets: 'You want to annotate my note-book? Oh, certainly!'—but fortunately there was no occasion to ask Shakespeare's leave. Shakespeare had been dead nearly fifty years. He was as remote from the sixteen-sixties as Tennyson from the nineteen-sixties. Allardyce Nicholl says in his essay on 'Dryden as an Adapter of Shakespeare': 'The Restoration beau did not mind viewing himself as he was, nor did he mind viewing impossibilities of love and honour and goodness; what he objected to was seeing before him on the stage what he might have been—' a remark that is a searchlight turned upon the Restoration age.

At the end of 1660 Davenant had already been given the right of 'making fit' nine plays of Shakespeare. They held that *Macbeth* and *Julius Caesar* in particular needed polishing. So they polished them. As for their operations on *The Tempest*—but Dr Samuel Johnson has already said all that is necessary on that head. Add a comment? As well try to rival the extremity of the skies. The Titan rolls himself about and

98

rumbles: there is an effect of lightning; then comes the pelting of the pitiless storm:

'The result of the conjunction of these two powerful minds was that to Shakespeare's monster Caliban is added a sister monster, Sicorax: and a woman who, in the original play, has never seen a man is, in this, brought acquainted with a man who has never seen a woman.'

Flash—crash! And so to thy cold bed and warm thee!

But the Dryden-Davenant improvements seem to have pleased Restoration audiences. They certainly pleased Dryden; though he was careful to give honour to his co-author; for Dryden, who did not love or even like easily, had a genuine admiration for Davenant. 'I found him of so quick a fancy that nothing was proposed to him in which he could not suddenly produce a thought extremely pleasant and surprising.'

The two powerful minds must of course share responsibility for the Shakespearean mass-murders, a practice which continued until our own times and is not yet ended. If I choose to think that the greater poet bore the greater blame, it is because I cannot love Dryden as I love Davenant. Something about Davenant charms me—I think it is the man's own happy nature.

But in fairness it must be told that once Davenant went quite mad and combined *Measure for Measure* with *Much Ado About Nothing*. This is in every way a shocking affair, and I would rather not talk about it. It is much better to turn to those fascinating prose poems which purport to be stage directions for the Inigo Jones masques, or to enjoy the country freshness of his lyrics. There is one at least which will never fade.

> 'The lark now leaves his watry nest
>   And climbing, shakes his dewy wings;
> He takes this window for the east;
>   And to implore your light, he sings:—
> "Awake, awake, the morn will never rise,
> Till she can dress her beauty at your eyes."

99

> The merchant bows unto the seaman's star,
>   The ploughman from the sun his season takes;
> But still the lover wonders what they are
>   Who look for day before his mistress wakes.
> "Awake, awake, break through your veils of lawn!
> Then draw your curtains, and begin the dawn." '

'Dewy wings!' That could only have been written by a man who can identify himself with any living creature. You know that he has imaginatively felt the sensation of dew on feathers and the need to preen them, just as Shakespeare felt the poor beetle's pang, and it is Davenant's cleansing virtue as a poet. When he was working in the theatre as a compelled craftsman he was as coarse as his refined age required, and to us as boring. But the body of his independent work, especially the half-private poems published after his death, suggests that here was a creature who had, in flashes and gleams, something wilder, wiser and more lasting than a mere stage talent. In his youth he had seen Shakespeare plain, had stopped and spoken with him, and Shakespeare had spoken with him again. The experience had lightly marked him.

He died at the age of sixty-two, still young at heart. He was buried in Poets' Corner; but Aubrey, who loved him, says wistfully: 'Methought that a laurel should have been set on his coffin—which was not done.'

Before his death Davenant was planning a new theatre nearer the river, a stone's throw from the present Guildhall School of Music. The Duke's Company, headed by Betterton, moved there in 1671, and the theatre, which was soon called The Queen's, looked like becoming a dangerous rival to Drury Lane; for the Thames waterways were as much used as the roads, and the place was convenient for City and Court alike. Then a worse disaster overtook the King's Company: the Drury Lane playhouse was burnt down, and the homeless actors were glad to huddle into the abandoned theatre in Lincoln's Inn Fields while the new Drury Lane Theatre was being built.

100

It was reopened in 1674—Christopher Wren was the architect—and Davenant's playhouse was once more abandoned and that time reconverted into a tennis-court; for the Duke's Company was apparently settled for good in their new home by the river. But the Queen's was big and expensive to run—a gaudy house, Dryden called it—and theatre entertainment in general was temporarily under a cloud. Finally the two companies joined forces, once more at the Lane, and the Queen's was acquired by one Christopher Rich, the chief patentee of the Lane.

Rich was a scrimping theatrical Scrooge, and he treated his actors so badly that finally Betterton, the head of the profession, led a revolt. He and his company formed a sort of proto-Equity, and when better terms could not be wrung out of Christopher Skinflint an appeal was made to the King and Queen. King William was no great theatre-goer; but Queen Mary had the Stuart passion for the theatre, and Betterton was—Betterton. So the King saw the deputation himself—it was in a sense a meeting of monarchs —and as nobody has ever at any time accused King William of being a fool, he soon solved the problem by giving the actors leave and licence to return to their old home, Davenant's playhouse in Lincoln's Inn Fields, leaving Rich and the other patentees in disgruntled possession of the Lane.

This is the generally accepted version of the story, though Cibber's version does not entirely agree. But Cibber was one of the younger actors who knew that the defection of their leaders was their chance. So they stuck to the Lane: and Rich, with what was left him, made a tremendous effort to reopen ahead of the rebels.

In this he succeeded by nearly a month. But the gods were on Betterton's side, and that thirtieth of April the delayed reopening of the Lincoln's Inn House was a triumphant one. It was not only the first night of the great return: it was also the first night of Congreve's *Love for Love*.

Valentine was played by Betterton, the Betterton whose
artistry the jealous Dryden trusted so implicitly that he
allowed him to cut a thousand lines out of one of his plays.
The beautiful Mrs Bracegirdle played Angelica, and Mrs
Barry, Rochester's mistress and pupil, played Mrs Frail:
and Mrs Bracegirdle and Mrs Barry were the most famous
actresses of their time. Ben the sailor was in the hands
of Doggett the Irish comedian, and it is said that Congreve
tailored the part for him. The house was packed, and King
William appeared in the Royal Box.

The Lincoln's Inn company must have had a thrilling
foreknowledge of success to help them through the first
night nerves. They had triumphed over the commercial
entrepreneurs, had been justified by the King and backed in
their new venture by the supreme wit of the stage. Betterton, King William, Congreve: these were three reliable
cushions to lean back against. Added to that they were home
again in their own luck-bringing theatre, Davenant's
theatre, and they knew that the all-important 'town' wished
them well, and that the footmen in the gallery concurred.

All these undercurrents of hope, excitement and senti-
ment are expressed in the Prologue and the Epilogue.
Betterton talked of the play they were about to see; but
he remained properly and charmingly professional.

> 'We hope there's something that may please each taste,
> And though of homely fare we make the feast,
> Yet you will find variety at least.
> There's humour, which for cheerful friends we got,
> And for the thinking party there's a plot.
> We've something too to gratify ill nature,
> (If there be any here) and that is, satire—'

But when Mrs Bracegirdle came forward to speak Rowe's
Epilogue she talked familiarly, as to old friends, of the
delight that everyone was feeling behind the scenes at
being back home in the old Davenant playhouse.

'Sure Providence at first designed this place
To be the players' refuge in distress;
For still in every storm they all run hither,
As to a shed that shields 'em from the weather.'

Then she amused them by comparing herself and the company to lost souls who, after death, have to wander from shape to shape till they find human accommodation once more.

'Methinks, we players resemble such a soul;
That does from bodies, *we* from houses stroll. . . .
And thus, our audience, which did once resort
To shining theatres to see our sport,
Now finds us tossed into a tennis-court. . . .
I vow I don't much like this transmigration,
Strolling from place to place by circulation—'

Then, being what she was, she must have suddenly by a mere change of voice brought a lump into more than one throat.

'But we can't fear, since you're so good to save us,
That you have only set us up—to leave us.
Thus from the past, we hope for future grace
I beg it—
And some here know I have a begging face.
Then pray continue this your kind behaviour.
For a clear stage won't do, without your favour.'

What a woman! What a play! What a first night! *What* a first night!

The success can't have pleased Christopher Skinflint, who was not making money at the Lane, though he stuck there, cheating and cheeseparing, for another ten years. The Betterton group in 1705 reconstructed itself under Congreve and Vanbrugh and moved to the Haymarket, and Rich snapped up the once more abandoned Lincoln's Inn playhouse as a retreat for a rainy day. The rainy day came

103

four years later, when his actors and the patentees finally managed to dislodge him by getting the Lord Chamberlain to close the theatre and kill the patent.

Drury Lane, of course, was shortly reopened under a new licence, when it was found that Rich, characteristically, had taken with him everything that could be scrounged or stolen. Drury Lane's recovery took time; but under Cibber, Doggett and Wilks it became prosperous, and in the days of Garrick, glorious.

But Christopher Rich was not beaten. Just before his death he set about rebuilding the old, rackety Davenant playhouse in the Fields. After his death it was opened by his son, John Rich, who made a fortune by putting on *The Beggar's Opera*, and with the proceeds finally avenged his father and tweaked the nose of the Lane. For he bought a site on the very edge of the Garden between Bow Street and the Piazza, and there he built Drury Lane's lasting rival, the theatre which, twice rebuilt, is today our own Royal Opera House.

And now you have followed every zigzag of the filament spun between the garden on Avon and the Garden on Thames.

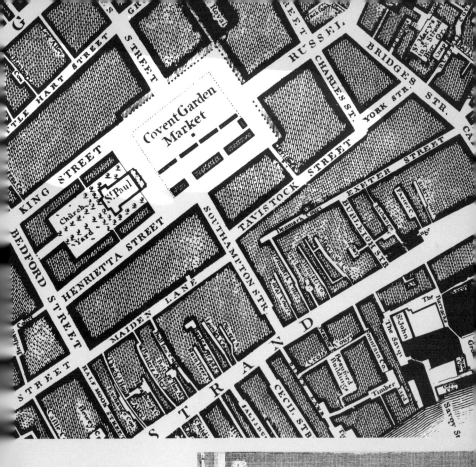

Georgian

VI

More Opera

John Rich was as shrewd a businessman as his father, but
wiser, a born pro' and a fine actor, though he was perhaps
the only man in the London of his day who believed that
he could play tragedy. But by all accounts he was excellent
in comedy and a great Harlequin—the greatest that had
ever been or would be according to a generation that knew
not Marcel Marceau. A contemporary once watched him
rehearsing the hatching of Harlequin by the heat of the
sun out of a gigantic pantomime egg, and calls it 'a masterpiece in dumb show, from the first chipping of the egg, his
receiving of motion, his feeling of the ground, his standing
upright, to his quick Harlequin trip round the empty shell.
Through the whole progression every limb had its tongue
and every motion a voice.'

He must have been pretty good; for it reads like a description of Marcel Marceau in his mime of a statue coming
to life in a public park, waking, descending, contemplating,
and then becoming in turn each member of the crowd, at
one moment two old ladies knitting, at another a pair of
lovers or a child, or a balloon-seller, or a woman with a dog.

Rich at any rate was a sufficiently remarkable figure to
catch the attention of Pope. Attention, not appreciation.
In every nation there occasionally arise poets who are
among other things the expression of their century. In
England we have had four such emanations—Chaucer,
Shakespeare, Pope and Dickens. Each could look with
affection at a cross-section of his fellow-men and, by adding
something of himself, create an immortal figure.

Chaucer's choice was the English trading, travelling

citizen, and he created the Wife of Bath. Shakespeare looked at the Elizabethan tavern-intellectual and created a Falstaff. Dickens looked at the Victorian white-collar failure and gave us Micawber. If he had cared to look with a kindly eye upon the eccentric Covent Garden manager accepting and rejoicing in his peculiar accent, his habit of calling everybody 'Mister', his pretty ladies and his twenty-seven cats, Pope could have given us a fourth wonder of portraiture. He had only to breathe his own breath into the figure, the poet's breath of life.

But there was not enough love in him for that. He could not recognize in the coarse histrion with an eye to the main chance a fellow artist.

> 'See now what Dulness and her sons admire,
> See what the charms that smite the simple heart
> Not touched by nature and not reached by art.'

All he saw was a Black Sorcerer, who had the impudence to create a 'new world to Nature's laws unknown' and what was more impudent still, a wordless world—which made him a blasphemer; for the Word created all things, and with words the poet recreates them. Therefore to write of 'groves which shine with silver frost' is a legitimate evocation of beauty; but to debauch popular imagination with paper snow is a devilish idea. So Pope kicked poor Harlequin into the Dunciad.

> 'Immortal Rich, how calm he sits at ease
> Mid snows of paper and fierce hail of peas,
> And, proud his mistress' orders to perform,
> Rides in the whirlwind and directs the storm.'

Magnificent invective—but Pope missed his mark. It was not dullness that made Rich immortal: it was originality.

His absurd genius is indicated in an hilarious sketch of the time labelled *Rich's Glory*. It purports to represent the manager's state entry into his newly built Covent Garden Theatre.

A procession of actors follow an open carriage drawn by men dressed as pantomime beasts. Pierrot and Columbine sit at the back, and Rich himself, dressed as Harlequin, is on the box, waving a banner with 'Rich for Ever' printed upon it. A bewigged gentleman precedes them, riding upon another man's shoulders. Behind them is Rich's coach, looking like an Emmet railway carriage, and the whole Comus crew heads for the huge, shadowy entrance to the theatre in the Piazza. In the foreground a few friends applaud with servile enthusiasm; but on the far side of Rich and his procession the spectators are vague nonentities, and behind them the Covent Garden square is painted like a back-cloth with St Paul's in the middle and bland streets to right and left. There are brick booths on the south side, and the tall pillar with the sundial rears up in the centre of the square; but not even a stray dog breaks the Garden's expression of total disinterest in Rich's Glory. It is a fair guess that the painter is having his private joke at Rich's expense; for there must have been a big crowd; the Market adores a novelty.

Voltaire was once mobbed by loiterers because he looked too French for them; till Voltaire sprang on to a doorstep and thence harangued them—oh to have heard that outpouring!—on the charm and valour of the English. They were so completely won over that, Frenchman or no Frenchman, they bore him back to his lodgings in Maiden Lane on their shoulders. The Market also enjoys meeting any figure that it has seen on the stage or the films or the telly.

'Got your clean curtains up, Miss Dane, I see. Who's coming tonight?'

Once when Sybil Thorndike came peering along Tavistock Street having, as usual, forgotten my number, a form rose from the nearest flower-dump and accosted her masterfully. 'I know who you are, and I know where you're going. You're Dame Sybil Thorndike, and you're going to see Miss Dane,' and with that escorted her to my entry.

Friendly—the streets in the theatre areas are always friendly. Once, as I turned into Coventry Street at the end of the war, I saw a jeep with Eisenhower standing up in it surrounded by servicemen, all laughing and talking at once. He and they were completely unaware of the crowds who watched, and the crowds didn't mind. They weren't there to intrude. They had only stopped to watch because they liked Eisenhower.

But the sport-heroes rank highest. Aubrey Smith taught me that lesson. Sir Aubrey Smith, who died in the 'fifties when he was over ninety, was a much-loved actor who had been a matinee idol in his youth. I first saw him in 1905 playing with Ellen Terry and the young Irene Vanbrugh in Barrie's *Alice Sit by the Fire.* I was a student at the Slade school in the days when he was one of the big London stars, and I thought he looked just like the painter Henry Tonks, who taught at the Slade and was then the central figure of my universe. The longing that all youngsters feel for the adventure of the stage was not lessened by almost nightly attendance at one or other of the galleries— not art but theatre galleries. There were moments when I even wondered what it would feel like to be an actress and play the Vanbrugh parts, and yet more fantastic moments when I wondered what it would feel like to be a dramatist and write parts for the Aubrey Smiths. But I'd have been contented to get a theatrical poster accepted. Anything to be in touch with theatre!

Sometimes wishes actually come true. In due course I made nice pocket-money out of theatre-posters, and later I did go on the stage and play Vanbrugh parts in seaside towns, and later still did at last write a play. Aubrey Smith played in it and was as delightful to work with as he had been to watch from the gallery sixteen years earlier in romantic, long forgotten comedies—*A Merry Devil*— *The Morals of Marcus*—leaves on the wind, all of them.

In the 'thirties his health forced him to settle in California, where he became a fixed star of the films. He and

Lady Smith used to come home now and again on a visit, though, and one day, after lunch with me in Covent Garden, their car was late. Aubrey Smith, with his usual vigorous impatience, insisted on going down into Tavistock Street to look for it himself. 'Aubrey! It's *barely* three.' But he won the argument by not hearing it, and we all trailed after him down the dark, twisty stairs and along the passage with the torn oilcloth.

I had not acquired a front-door in those days, and as usual there were a few porters and customers lingering in the entry after the shop hours. They scattered politely to make room for us; but they did not go away, and presently they were joined by other market-men till there was a small crowd. I knew most of them, but they weren't bothering about me: they were watching Aubrey Smith. He must have been well over seventy even then; but he still had the carriage and the air of an energetic captain-of-the-games and that young look which is so characteristic of the deaf. There he stood in the middle of the road, slanted forward a little like the Epstein statue of Smuts at Westminster, looking the wrong way for his car, which was meantime approaching from the other end of the street. He was totally unconscious of observers.

'Aubrey!' his wife called, very loudly as she always had to do, and the name, echoing back from the Covered Way, settled it. I heard an old man say impatiently to an open-mouthed youngster: 'Who *is* it? It's *Round-the-Corner Smith!*' Then and only then did I remember that Aubrey Smith, that fine actor, had been known to thousands who never went near the theatre as a cricketer. They called him 'Round-the-Corner-Smith' because when he was bowling he would begin his run either from deep mid-off or from deep mid-on behind the umpire, and—according to W. G. Grace—'it is highly disconcerting when the bowler suddenly appears from behind the umpire,' that is, from round the corner. Aubrey Smith must have liked his nickname, for his house at the top of Cold Water Canyon, with its views from San Fernando Valley to the Pacific ocean and its wholly English garden, was called 'Round the Corner'.

I had forgotten—or never knew—the cricket angle; but the Market hadn't forgotten, and at once he was nearly swept off his feet by a smiling, excited crowd of elderly men. There was a flurry of talk and laughter, then the car honked behind his back and they all turned him round and hoisted him in. He grabbed at his quiet wife, as usual taking old-fashioned pains to see that she was comfortable. Then he was borne away.

'Nobody like him!' somebody said to no one in particular; but as the men dispersed one or two turned to me with: 'Thank you, Miss Dane.'

I went soberly back; realizing at last that star-quality is not confined to the theatre. I didn't know mid-on from mid-off: the Market didn't know heroics from ham; but the Market knew an artist when it saw one, and I knew an artist when I saw one. As we were all looking at the same man, who was to say which was the more important—the acting or the bowling? The art or the sport?

It was hard to take; but I had to concede that if Ellen Terry was to remain a potent memory, then I must also learn to prize the memory of W. G. Grace seen through netting—a red-hot W. G. Grace in white flannels with an enormous square beard that made him look like Conan Doyle's Professor Challenger. But then I thought about the fun I should have as an old lady of at least seventy-five. When the younger generations talked about cricket, sure that I was deaf, blind and incapable of following the conversation, I should say: 'It's long before your times, of course, but *I* once saw W. G. Grace.' Then I'd clinch it with: 'And I knew Round-the-Corner Smith quite well.'

The last time I saw him he was climbing into a plane to attend some special cricketing function five hundred miles away. He was well over ninety, but he was *going* strong, the handsome old man with his great beak and straight look. The Market was right—nobody like him.

To return to John Rich and his immortality; for he also has become immortal—half immortal at any rate—by virtue of his showman's love of a gamble. He took a chance with John Gay and another when he built the Covent Garden Theatre, and was each time well paid in the coins of this world; but he achieved immortality when he took a chance with Handel.

When he opened his theatre in Covent Garden the public was mad about Italian opera in spite of the James Millers who refused to find anything good in foreign music.

'In days of old, when Englishmen were—men,
Their music, like themselves, was grave and plain. . . .
But now . . .
A hundred various instruments combine,
And foreign songsters in the concert join:—
The shrill ton'd fiddle, and the warbling flute,
The grave bassoon, deep base, and twinkling lute. . . .
All league, melodious nonsense to dispense,
All give us Sound, and Show, instead of Sense;
In unknown tongues mysterious dullness chant,
Make love in tune, or thro' the gamut rant.'

Now John Rich had early learned the showman's lesson —find out what audiences want and give them the best in that kind. Whom should he get? There was only one answer in the seventeen-thirties—Handel.

Handel had arrived in England in 1710. He settled in London and proceeded to fulfil his destiny there as the great creative force in English music for the rest of the century. But for many years the general public knew him best as a composer of operas and his life and his work were inevitably painfully affected by the shifting moods of Grub Street and the coffee-houses.

Also, by one of those furtive arrangements of Providence which we call Chance, a second creative force came into

existence in 1710—the critical journalism of Addison and
Steele. Steele had already prepared the ground in *The
Tatler*, and on March 1st, 1710, Addison penned the three
opening words that were to guide their joint policy in *The
Spectator*: 'I have observed—'

By their humanity, charm, sly sense of fun and power
to entertain and yet edify their readers, these two men
of genius—good men—were to guide English taste and
influence English manners and morals very much as
Handel guided and influenced English music. Both men
hated extremes, though perhaps dislike is a better word;
for to Addison at any rate 'hated' would have been an
exaggeration and therefore a misuse of language. Inevitably one of their targets was Italian opera, because
of its scenic and other absurdities. They also ran a patriotic
campaign against the use of Italian: opera should be sung in
English. But the translation had to be a sensitive one; for as
The Spectator explained, he sought to protect the language
of music as well as the English language.

'I remember an Italian verse that ran thus, word for word:

"And turned my rage to pity,"

which the English, for rhyme's sake, translated:

"And into pity turned my rage."

By this means the soft notes that were adapted to pity in Italian
fell upon the word "rage" in English, and the angry sounds
that were tuned to "rage" in the original were made to express
"pity" in the translation.'

But Handel, who all his life spoke broken English, could
hardly have understood why Addison was offended—and
who knows if he ever looked into *The Spectator*?

The Spectator's sense of fitness was also troubled when
Italian singers sang their parts in their own language
while the rest of the cast sang in English. What he really
wanted was a complete Anglicization of opera with libretto
and score arranged to fit 'the humours of our language'.

112

Another dislike was the immoderate use of spectacle. When Handel's production of *Rinaldo* was put on at the Haymarket in 1711, *The Spectator* pretended to feel cheated because 'the King of Jerusalem is obliged to come from the city on foot instead of being drawn in a triumphant chariot with white horses, as my opera-book promised me.' Nor did it please him when the public was promised that cages full of sparrows should enter towards the end of a first act and fly about the stage. But nothing has cured the public of its passion for performing live-stock—no, not in two hundred years. I once saw Mrs Patrick Campbell, moving dazed through Hall Caine's melodrama, *The Bondman*. She was surrounded by sheep.

But if producers' folly was mocked by the two reformers, folly in the pit and boxes was not spared either.

'Our great grandchildren will be very curious to know why their forefathers used to sit together like an audience of foreigners in their own country to hear whole plays acted before them in a tongue which they did not understand. It does not want any great measure of sense to see the ridicule of this most monstrous practice.'

That practice has also survived, and so has the panto-mime element in opera at which *The Spectator* also poked fun.

'I cannot omit doing justice to the Boy who had the direction of the two painted dragons and made them spit fire and smoke. I saw indeed little wanting to render his whole action complete—I mean the keeping his head a little lower and hiding his candle.'

Again the crusade failed: directors slip up today just as they did under Queen Anne. Watching the *Alcina* first night at Covent Garden last year I felt a Spectatorly irritation when I caught glimpses of a shoulder and draperies behind the rocks of the revolving islet in the centre of the stage and realized (to the destruction of all illusion) that Miss Sutherland was waiting to be swung round into the next scene. Sutherland and Handel satisfied most of us: why had we to be shown a ride on a merry-go-round as well?

Alcina was one of the many operas Handel wrote specially for the Garden when he moved there from the Haymarket in 1734. It had a reasonable success, for it ran eighteen nights and was twice briefly revived. But the public was fickle, opera ceased to pay, and after little more than two years Handel was forced to retire, sick from overwork and almost ruined.

His greatest achievements were still ahead of him; but that he could not know. He knew only in those bitter years that within a twelve-month of his departure the theatre which he had faithfully served put on a burlesque—*The Dragon of Wantley*, and though the libretto reads dully enough today it was an immediate hit. But the British public has always enjoyed the dramatic excitement of turning its back suddenly on a popular idol.

> 'Bright beauties who in awful circle sit,
> And you, grave synod of the dreadful pit,
> And you, the upper tier of popgun wit,
> Pray ease me of my wonder, if you may.
> Is all this crowd barely to see the play?
> Or is't the poet's execution day?'

Dryden asserts that these lines were sent to him by 'an unknown hand' to be used as a prologue to one of his plays; but though it is always necessary to listen when Dryden speaks, it is not always necessary to believe what Dryden says. An unknown hand? Hm!

Anyway *The Dragon* ran for sixty-seven hilarious performances; and why should London audiences care that a genius lost all his savings and became seriously ill from overwork and worry?

When in trouble blame the management—but Handel does not seem to have resented his management's decisions; for he bequeathed to Rich the organ which he had built for use at Covent Garden. It remained in the theatre till the fire of 1808 destroyed it. A real gun had been fired, a legacy of Rich's obstinate theatricality, and a piece of wadding had smouldered till the whole place was ablaze.

Mrs Siddons says that all was well when she left, near midnight; but that by six in the morning, at which time her brother first heard of the disaster, he declared that 'it was so completely destroyed that you could not have known a building had stood there.' At the time of her letter she had clearly not learned of the lives sacrificed or the destruction of the Arne and Handel MSS; for she is the sort of woman who would have put them first. She speaks as a collector, even when speaking of her personal losses. 'I have lost everything, all my jewels and lace which I have been collecting for thirty years . . . all really fine and curious. I had a point veil which had been a toilette of the poor Queen of France, near five yards long. . . . In short everything I had in the world of stage ornament is gone, and literally not one vestige is left of all that has cost me so much time and money to collect.'

But it is a statement, not a complaint. She was not a complainer. Characteristically she turns to the next job. 'We are to act at the Opera,' (she means Drury Lane, then devoted to music), 'and next Monday I shall attempt the character of Lady Randolph.'

She had humility. She says 'attempt' when the part is already one of her triumphs. She adds—after that awful night—'My head is confused. I scarce know what I write—' but again her conclusion is characteristic. 'Everybody is good and kind, and please God we shall still do well.'

It is a strange thing that the Royal Opera House has always doled out ill-luck as impartially as it doles out triumphs. Like the Commendatore, it sooner or later lays its heavy hand on all its servants, and they are led away— into nothingness or immortality according to their quality. It is not likely that *The Dragon of Wantley* will ever be seen again—the libretto is yawningly dull. But Handel is

115

still Handel, and *Alcina* has been revived three times in the last ten years.

It was given in the 'fifties by the Handel Opera Society with the new-risen star, Joan Sutherland, in the name-part. Five years later the Royal Opera Company from Stockholm put on the opera at Covent Garden, and in 1962 it was revived again, with Sutherland once more singing the part of Alcina. This time the opera was directed by Zeffirelli, who also designed the sets and costumes.

Zeffirelli's *Romeo and Juliet*, staged at the Vic, had already made theatre history and had been followed by a superb romantical production of Mozart's *Don Giovanni* at the Garden; so when a Zeffirelli production of *Alcina* was announced people naturally expected another stage miracle. But miracles wouldn't be miracles if they happened regularly.

The *Alcina* production was architecturally splendid. The pillars of the vast hall disappeared in the distance, the costumes were rich and flamboyant, the dances sufficiently entertaining, the acting impeccable. Zeffirelli gave all that he is renowned for giving, and the evening began as an enchantment; but the end of it was a long time in coming; for though the music poured out as splendidly as a river in flood and the singing was gallant and sometimes lovely, it was hard to believe that we were seeing anything remotely like the *Alcina* that Handel's audiences saw.

An opera is a combination of all seven arts—music, singing, dancing, story-telling, architecture, painting and the written word, and if an audience suspects that the director is bored by even one of the components it will get restive before the evening ends.

Zeffirelli's approach showed at once that he was bored by the story; for he had written another one round it, the story of a nobleman who watches an entertainment staged in the centre of his great hall. It was Theseus and his Court, shifted to an age of elegance, watching a musical merry-go-round.

116

It was an ingenious idea brilliantly executed, but it was hard on the performers; for they found themselves required to play two parts at once. At one moment they were sophisticated Court singers perfectly at home in the splendid setting, and at the next they were impersonating fantastic figures of mediaeval romance. Magic was the theme of the opera, and the music and the singing was often magical; but the direction stayed outside the enchanted circle and perpetually destroyed the illusion that Handel's music and the singers' voices were attempting to create. Towards the end I found myself playing with the idea of, say, Tippetts's *Midsummer Marriage* performed at an Edwardian garden party in the grounds of Buckingham Palace with the players on intimate terms with royalty, and the guests occasionally joining in a little folk-dancing: and I went home cross.

Which was ungrateful; for it had not merely been an opportunity to hear an opera seldom performed, but to hear Joan Sutherland. She sang like a mocking-bird on a moonlight night, which is the loveliest sound I know. I got much the same pleasure from listening to her as years ago when, once or twice, I heard Melba sing.

Perhaps there are two sorts of great singers, the Voices and the Skin-Changers. The Skin-Changers are the born impersonators whose voices crown their acting gifts. Catalani, Chaliapine, Callas: these are all Skin-Changers.

But the Sutherlands and the Melbas are Voices. With careful staging they become sufficiently effective visually; but they act with their voices, they beglamour through their voices, they make the audience laugh or shiver by means of their voices. It is a different art. The Voices are music, and the rest of the equipment—looks, capacity to impersonate, age, figure and so on—doesn't matter, mustn't matter; though much more help is given to them today than was given in Victorian times. Old photographs tell us as much. The dresses are less cruel, it is no longer taken for granted that a respectable female singer should look like a cottage-loaf and a male singer like a tin-baked one. Large, seal-like ladies no longer swing through the air with the greatest of ease. They have dieted, and their vehicles are less swoopy. Neither are pantomime effects so frequent, though they still occur. John Rich would have shaken his head over the snake in the recent Klemperer production of *The Magic Flute* and called a rehearsal at ten sharp to teach it how to wriggle.

But the biggest change of the last sixty years is in acting standards, which has come in with the new younger directors. I once heard Melba and Caruso sing in *La Boheme*, and when I heard it again with Victoria de los Angeles I could hardly believe it was the same opera.

Melba was a Voice. It was such an exquisite voice that at the time it didn't seem to matter that the middle-aged figure standing in the doorway of the attic-studio looked like a housekeeper saying: 'What would you like for lunch?' But when Victoria de los Angeles stood in the doorway, she was Mimi. The story came alive, and Melba, as an actress, was blotted out. Only the remembrance of the Voice remained, the Voice which had had an all but visual beauty, as a bough of double-cherry has a beauty that is all but sound.

Yet off the stage Melba was broadly of the theatre. I met her once just after the First World War at a dinner-party given by an American publisher. We all met in an impersonal sitting-room at the Savoy: the evening was chilly, and the Thames and the Embankment Gardens could hardly be seen for mist. The company was literary, and I was new to that sort of gathering. I was introduced to one or two gods, but hadn't the nerve to be talkative. Cocktails came. They didn't help.

Suddenly a bustle in the doorway—Melba was entering all in one movement as if on roller-skates. She wore a dress of scarlet gauze liberally spangled with minute dewdrops. She was stoutish. She had eyes like a hawk or a head-mistress, and they at once took in the room and the

118

situation. She beamed inclusively, missing nobody, and from that moment the party was a party. She was a heavenly woman that evening, jocund, gleaming, wicked. We were her ninepins, and she bowled us over one after the other.

When we went down to the restaurant for dinner she began to clown, shamelessly and endearingly. A new dish was brought to her and she was told that it had been specially invented for her that very evening and was to be named after her. She was delighted. The surrounding tables stared, fascinated, till she flung her napkin over her face and besought her host to 'stop them!' I have never seen anyone enjoy herself nor make others enjoy themselves so much.

But she wanted all of us, our whole attention, our united admiration, and unluckily I had been placed next to an elder god whose books I knew by heart, and I suppose I had got a little too much absorbed in him and his charm. For suddenly Melba wailed across the table: 'I've been telling my best story, and there's Clemence Dane won't look at me, and isn't even listening.'

She won, the smiling, rollicking she-egoist. There was only one thing to do—surrender, and I did, and he did, and we all did, and enjoyed her more than ever. She was such wonderful theatre as a human being that it was impossible to believe that three hours earlier one had thought of her solely, and with awe, as a Voice.

VII

Rehearsals

Rehearsals! The creative excitement of rehearsals never stales, though no dramatist with practical experience of life in the theatre ever expects his play to resemble what he has seen in his mind's eye as he wrote it. For he, in the tense creative months, has already worked out for himself every minute detail. He can tell you if a table is two inches to the right or left of the door at the back, and whether that door ought to creak or not as it opens. He knows when the lights should dim, and times with passionate exactitude the lighting of a cigarette. If he has 'seen' the love-scene at the left end of the sofa he cannot be happy if it is played across an armchair on the right. He hears inside his head the pitch of every phrase. He knows that one actor must move like Horace Walpole skating into Lady Ossory's drawing-room, while another must slouch like Caliban.

Then he comes to rehearsal. There he finds that the director has re-arranged all the furniture because of the position of the property-room. He finds that his cast, whom he adores and resents, have their own notions of how the characters—his characters—should behave, and that these notions are not his. He discovers that *all* players put 'ands' and 'buts' and 'wells' before his carefully balanced sentences. The business that he has so carefully worked out is ignored and new business is invented which he finds an outrage.

And so, for the first three days at least, he becomes Bayes, the eternal Bayes, with interludes of Niobe weeping for her children.

Then, if he has a sense of humour and practical experience

of how actors work, he begins to enjoy the new views, the new approaches, the new interpretations, and settles for it that at the end of the all-absorbing, destructive, enriching rehearsal period he will see on a public stage, joyously if it's a success, with desolation if it is a failure, a play with which he has had something to do, but which is not his play. Then he settles down, the eternal optimist, to write another.

There are exceptions. I once wrote a piece in collaboration with the composer Richard Addinsell, which was put on in New York with Stephen Haggard and Judith Anderson, and ran for a mere six weeks. But that was the only time in forty years of theatre that I have ever been able to say: 'This is what we wanted, exactly as we wanted it,' and the pleasure of the experience was so intense that failure didn't seem to matter.

I wonder how often the members of a company can look at each other after a performance and without paying compliments say in the manner of Nero Wolfe: 'Satisfactory!' I saw that happen once, and it was impressive.

Noel Coward's play had gone into rehearsal the week before the war. It was called *Present Laughter* and was the lightest of frivolous comedies. Some of us thought it his best since *Private Lives*. Even among the major anxieties of that strange pre-war week it was rather sad to get a telephone call from the author over breakfast: 'I suppose you've seen the papers. Would you like to come to rehearsal at ten-thirty? It's the only chance you'll ever have now of seeing the show.'

I went, expecting a bare stage, make-shift chairs, chalk-lines and hysteria.

Not at all. The set was up, the properties were all to hand, the company was already word-perfect. The performance was so smooth that the actors might have been playing half-way through a run, and as the first scene of the second act drew to its absurd climax one forgot everything and began to shake with laughter at the two super-

121

egoists on the sofa. One was played by Judith Campbell and the other by Noel Coward.

GARRY: How was the Toscanini concert?
JOANNA: Glorious. He played the Eighth and the Seventh.
GARRY: [*moving below the settee and spacing his words whilst arranging a cushion*] Personally—I always—prefer—the Fifth.
[*He sits beside her.*]
JOANNA: I like the Ninth best of all.
GARRY: [*laying his hand on hers*] Nothing like the dear old Ninth.
[*He picks up her hand and kisses the palm.*]
JOANNA: I love Covent Garden, don't you? It's so uncompromising.
GARRY: I love the Albert Hall much, much more.
JOANNA: I wonder why. I always find it depressing.
GARRY: [*slipping his arm beneath her*] Not when they're doing *Hiawatha*, surely?
JOANNA: [*putting her arm round his neck, dreamily*] Even then.
GARRY: [*with his mouth close to hers*] I won't hear one word against the Albert Hall.

Suddenly a voice from the wings called out: 'The news! Time for the news!' There was the click of a radio-switch, and a voice rang out—

'The adjustment of differences by negotiation and not by force, a respect for the pledged word—these are the principles which seem to us vital for the peaceful and orderly life of nations, and these are the things, nothing less, which if trouble comes we are concerned to defend.'

When the radio switched off there was a moment of silence, followed by a general sigh. Then, without comment, Miss Campbell slipped back onto the sofa, and Noel Coward picked up his line: 'I won't hear a word against the Albert Hall.' War, everybody knew, was now certain; but the rehearsal continued flawlessly to the last assured line and the characteristic *Private Lives* type exit. Satisfactory!

Another rehearsal sticks in my mind. Lewis Casson and Sybil Thorndike once put on *The Cenci* for a brief season at the Leicester Square Empire for the sufficient reason that they wanted to. They have the Quixote streak. The part of Cenci himself had been created by Robert Farquharson, strange and fey, that season it was played by Hubert Carter, who had immense brute force and a huge voice. Sybil Thorndike played Beatrice. I was concerned in the show because the Cassons had asked me to speak a foreword.

The rehearsal which I found so memorable happened early. We were all gathered on the bare, draughty stage of the Empire. There were no sets and no props. Sybil Thorndike, who had a bad cold, was wearing the ancient knitted cardigan that every woman saves for such misfortunate days. It was green. So was her tweed skirt. Her hair was wild, and she was without make-up.

On the first night, of course, she wore sixteenth-century dress. It suited her, and her performance was deeply moving; but the moment—that rare moment when there is an actual transference of identity—came at that rehearsal, in the last scene, when the little group of broken victims are preparing for death on the scaffold, and the poetry that Shelley had poured into the play seemed to be concentrated in a tired woman wearing a green cardigan.

It is not a mere illusion of memory either; for this morning, May 15th of 1963, I found that I had left my volume of Shelley in London, and rang up Sybil Thorndike to check on the last lines.

She was in a breathless hurry. She and Sir Lewis were just off to a matinee of their poetry recital at the Haymarket, and I heard agitation in the background. 'Sybil, the car's at the *door*!'

'Oh Lewis, can't you tell him to wait just *one* minute! Are you there, Winifred? Here it is.' And then the lovely lines came to me over the telephone in all their grave agony of resignation:

> 'Here Mother, tie
> My girdle for me, and bind up this hair
> In any simple knot. Ay, that does well.
> And yours, I see, is coming down. How often
> Have we done this for one another? Now
> We shall not do it any more. My lord,
> We are quite ready. Well! 'Tis very well.'

The forty years had made no difference. The transference of identity was instantaneous and, over the casual telephone, once more deeply moving.

I used to wonder if such strange moments also happened at opera working-rehearsals. Until last year I had never seen one, though I had seen quite a lot of pre-first nights with big invited audiences. But such guests always refuse vodka. They are fruit-juice listeners. The performers wait in vain for the response that makes any stage performance, play or opera, come alive.

But once, before a mere handful of people, I saw an opera bewitched into life. The first night of Britten's *A Midsummer Night's Dream* at Covent Garden was an exciting one; but the dress-rehearsal held a day or so earlier was downright uncanny. The tiny audience sat in the stalls circle, and the sole tenant of the arena was a will o' the wisp John Gielgud wandering in the aisles. But the fact that the huge place was almost empty did not flatten the performance. It merely altered its quality as night air alters the scents of a garden.

The opera began in the wood near Athens—the set was realistic—the moonlight lay thick as snow—and almost at once the music began to create the illusion that the glade was alive and beginning to enlarge its boundaries, spreading out over the empty stalls, turning the seats into rocks and boulders and the aisles into dim rides. The

124

lovers' song is moving enough at performance; but at that rehearsal it moved one differently. It was such a lonely song sung in the huge, empty house. On the first night the house was full and the song was passionate, but the sense of loneliness had been banished. The smell of the night and the chill of dew was in the music, and 'I know a bank' was a familiar passage written in a new language. Again there was the most remarkable transference of an inner experience into exterior sound.

Music apart, one of the most effective moments was Geraint Evans's dalliance with Titania. He was less physically right than many Bottoms: he couldn't quite get rid of his own intelligent-leprechaun look; but he had bits of business when wearing the ass's head which were superbly funny. Once, having been drawn down by Titania's arms to sleep on her breast, he quite suddenly lifted that huge, long-eared head in a stare of questioning surprise—as a dog will do in an unfamiliar room, and the clumsy mask actually became alive and somehow touching. Again, in the morning when he had been released from the spell, Bottom suddenly gave an odd little kick with one leg as if the donkey in him were not yet outed—delicious character-acting.

But all these things happened at a perfected dress-rehearsal: no idea was to be gleaned from it of what went on at any *working* rehearsal of an opera. I have always wanted to know who came first at such times, conductor or director, and how much attention was paid to the librettist when he wasn't Shakespeare. Was it anything like the three-way tug-of-war in Strauss's *Capriccio*?

THE AUTHOR: First the words, then the music.
THE COMPOSER: First the music, then the words.
THE DIRECTOR: [*waking up*] Without me your works are— dead paper.

When Convent Garden put on the new *Don Giovanni* my chance to learn came; for I was allowed to watch two consecutive rehearsals. Zeffirelli was directing and had designed the sets and dresses.

Zeffirelli, as at least a thousand elderly theatregoers have already pointed out, is the Reinhardt of the 'sixties. His recent *Romeo and Juliet* at the Old Vic excited audiences very much as Reinhardt's *Oedipus* excited audiences at Covent Garden in 1912. No one present on that first night will ever forget what Reinhardt did to the nerves of the stalls in the first three minutes by a mere trick of sound. I stress the stalls, because I had never before been anywhere but in the gallery on a first night. But a solitary ticket had come my way, and there I was, in a marvellous seat, knowing nobody, but enjoying myself as only the young and stage-struck can. My evening dress was of white jap silk cut square at the neck. White flowers were worn in the hair. I saw nothing wrong with it at the time. It was a long while ago.

Everyone was surprised to find that the orchestra-pit had vanished, and that the proscenium-arch was un-curtained and filled by the vast bronze doors of a building with overwhelming Zeffirelli-type pillars and a flight of steps which led to an altar in the centre of the arena. For some time nothing happened. Late-comers squeezed in apologetically till every seat was filled. The audience mur-mured, rustled its programmes, re-arranged itself and gradually stopped talking, and after a while began to fidget. Still nothing happened.

From the gallery and the upper circles it had always been possible to get a fair impression of what the whole house is feeling; but sitting in the middle of the stalls I found that the impression was a much more limited one, and I won-dered if the growing tension was an illusion. But it was soon clear that people were fidgeting because of an infinitesima sense of discomfort, as if a hair were tickling. But it was a sound, a sound no louder than a grasshopper's lisp. It came from everywhere at once and was somehow menacing.

Heads began to turn. As the noise increased severa

people began to rise from their seats, and I thought there was going to be a panic. But at that moment a yelling mob tore in from every doorway and rushed down the aisles and passages to the altar at the foot of the steps. The Chorus had made its entrance.

It was an intensely exciting stage-effect. Equally exciting was the later scene where the blind priest warns Oedipus to let sleeping furies lie, and warns in vain. Martin Harvey stood on the steps, silhouetted against the red-bronze doors. The priest stood at the far end of the theatre, and the two actors, who both had fine voices, flung their questions and answers at each other across the spaces of the house like primeval giants hurling boulders from hill-top to hill-top.

Theatre in the round has by now made such excitements commonplace. That is the trouble about novelties. Once you know the trick the thrill is gone—which is where the author scores. The thrill never lessens however often Macbeth and his wife meet on the staircase:

MACBETH: I have done the deed.—Didst thou not hear a noise?
LADY MACBETH: I heard the owl scream and the crickets cry.
Did not you speak?
MACBETH: When?
LADY MACBETH: Now.
MACBETH: As I descended?
LADY MACBETH: Ay.
MACBETH: Hark!—'

This is not the director at work inventing stage-effects. It is the dramatist working directly on the audience's imagination, which is, I suppose, why non-actors who spend the best part of their lives in the theatre generally prefer a good rehearsal to a good first night. They know that there will often be one rehearsal which is special and which happens when the actor has for the moment ceased to bother about his costume or his make-up and is, like Prospero, relying upon his own magical power.

That is the spectator's point of view. Young actors seldom

agree with it. That is natural, for they still need the trappings. They are like people learning to cycle, who can ride splendidly but haven't yet learnt to get on or get off. In his first book of reminiscences, *Early Stages*, John Gielgud relates how important it was to him as a very young actor to get out of himself into costume and make-up. He says:

'I imagine at rehearsals how I hope to look, but if my make-up comes out well at the first dress rehearsal, my confidence is increased a hundredfold. In the same way, the right clothes— especially in a part where they must be heavy and dignified— help me at once to find the right movements and gestures for the character. One's expression in a character part develops tremendously quickly after the first few times of making-up. Photographs taken at a dress rehearsal only show a kind of mask, a sketch of the actor's intention, just like his performance at an early rehearsal. Photograph him again after he has been acting the part for a fortnight, and the whole expression has deepened, and developed into something much more complete, revealing the mental conception of the part in the eyes and mouth, as well as in the lines and shadows that are painted over them.'

The passage was written when Gielgud was thirty-four. He is looking back to his Macbeth, which he played eight years earlier, and it is obvious that he is trying to record exactly how he felt and thought as a young player, and also that his views had still not changed.

But he has since made it clear that the need for grease-paint and costume is but a phase in a great actor's development; for nearly a quarter of a century later he put on a show called *The Seven Ages of Man*. He appeared as himself on the empty stage. He wore a dinner-jacket, and his make-up was no more than an adjustment to the lighting. He used some sort of unobtrusive support for his papers, and I think there was a chair. The background was red curtains.

Thus equipped he began with a few words of introduction and a line or two of linking comment between each scene to conjure up the principal figures of the Shakespearean canon.

The evening began thus, with the one man in modern clothes on the empty stage. But it ended—and nearly everyone with whom I discussed the scene reported the same thing—with the illusion that the stage was crowded with nine-foot-high figures in full costume. Mercutio made way for Hamlet—Richard—Leontes—Lear—Prospero, each after their moment retreating into the red shadows but never leaving the stage, till by the end of the evening it was so crowded with ghosts and entities that Gielgud himself vanished. He was still on the stage, obviously, but one didn't notice him, not, that is, till the curtains dropped for the last time and the spell was wound up. It was the most extraordinary piece of magicking. But throughout that creative evening Gielgud used no make-up and no costumes, which justified anyone in saying that it's worth getting in to a theatre rehearsal whenever you get the chance, for there is always the possibility of an experience like that of Job's friend, when the spirit passed before his face and the hair of his head stood up.

I had first heard *Don Giovanni* a year or so after the Boer War, and since then whenever I got the chance; but I had missed the Zeffirelli *Romeo and Juliet* so I was in a state of beautiful ignorance over what was likely to happen at these particular rehearsals.

Added to that the expert in shorthand who came with me had never heard the music and didn't know the story, and it's not easy to make notes in the dark house when you can't identify the figures on the stage and have to guess at the plot. Fortunately the traffic-jams were at their peak that February morning, so we had time between Chelsea and the Garden to run over the outline of the admittedly confusing libretto.

We began by getting it clear that the curtains part on a square in Seville at midnight. Leporello, Don Giovanni's factotum, is keeping watch. Don Giovanni has

E

broken into the Commendatore's house, hoping to seduce his daughter, Donna Anna. The two come out, struggling. The father rushes after them, and while Donna Anna wrenches herself free and goes for help there is a fight, the Commendatore is killed, and Don Giovanni escapes unrecognized.

So far, easy. But then there is a change of plot. Don Giovanni is pursued by another wronged heroine, Elvira. He escapes again, leaving her to be mocked by Leporello. Then comes a third plot, with Don Giovanni making love to a peasant girl, Zerlina, who is saved from him by Elvira. Then he is recognized and denounced by Donna Anna. Then there is a feast for the villagers, Zerlina is once more rescued, and Don Giovanni once more gets away—and so it goes on in a muddle of farce, tragedy and romance that nobody could take seriously in a play.

But this is an opera. There were once seven Powers who stood before the Throne and mediated between God and man, and the best loved of them all was called 'God Heals' or 'The Angel of the Spirit of Men'. Today the seven archangels have become the seven arts, and the Angel of the Spirit of Men is called Music.

Mozart, in the grip of that Power, transformed the petty creatures of the libretto. They became spirits of men—and women—while Don Giovanni himself, when he faced the statue of the dead man in the churchyard, had grown, like Faust, into an Everyman. Faust, in his intellectual greed, sold his soul to the devil: Don Giovanni, in his greed for sensation, invited Death to dinner—and Death accepted.

> 'Twelve of the clock, Don Juan!
> In came he,
> That shining, cold and tall authority,
> Whose marble lips smiled down on lips that pray,
> And took my hand, and I was led away.'

That settled, we went in to rehearsal.

To enter the Royal Opera House when it is vivid with

lights and conversation is always exciting; but it is much more exciting to slip into a seat at the side of the stalls-circle, when the huge auditorium is empty and there is only the one house-light up in the roof. If the spells are working it is like sitting on the floor of a universe looking up at the curves of space.

Then a glimmer of brilliant light shoots out suddenly between the crack in the curtains. It illuminates the crowned shields and reveals the rake of the huge stage. The rows of empty stalls begin to emerge like hedges out of a fog.

That morning there was a piano in the orchestra-pit, and a table was set in the main gangway about four rows from the back. There were two shrouded lamps on it and a pile of books and scripts, and round it dim figures sat and talked in undertones. I could make out the General Adminis-trator whom I knew and a smallish, alert figure whom I didn't know. His muffler strung out behind him like pig-tails whenever he dashed off to the stage-bridge. He turned out to be the director, Zeffirelli.

For a long while nothing happened: not that waiting was dull. Taking in details was as entertaining as a Fielding novel, comfortably briefing you about the whole situation before the story begins, but with a constantly increasing sense of tension till, suddenly and dramatically, all the lights went out. Still nothing happened till a girl in red came out between the glowing curtains. She was at once addressed by the table.

THE TABLE: [*impatiently*] What are we waiting for?
THE GIRL IN RED: [*unimpressed*] Artists.
THE TABLE: [*quenched*] Oh, how sad! [*hopefully*] Can't you chase them up?

At that moment two spotlights suddenly shone out of the pitch-darkness from somewhere in the third Heaven, one blue and one amber. The outer curtains lifted and revealed inner curtains which the lighting had turned to bronze

131

and ultramarine. Lady Eden's priceless Spanish leather screens must have looked much the same after Whistler had got at them with his glue and silver paint. The girl in red strolled towards the right and crossed over the orchestra-pit into the house by the stage-bridge—the longest bridge I had ever seen in a theatre. Then the inner curtains parted in turn to reveal nobly romantic architecture swimming in a gloom of gold and umber. On the left were huge pillars, on the right practical steps and a portico. The back of the stage was one enormous wrought-iron gate standing up against a midnight sky.

This beautiful and impressive set at once told the audience that the most ambiguous of all operas was going to be presented as a romantic tragedy set in a world that Velasquez invented and Goya fantasticalized; but that there was also to be gaiety. This was guaranteed by a crouching figure in a cloak and slouch-hat—the Leporello of Geraint Evans.

The piano hinted that it was time to begin; but instead of at once breaking into 'Here I'm working day and night—un-appreciated—out in all weathers—bad food—little sleep—' and so on, Geraint Evans rose and, addressing the distant table, began to say exactly what he felt about curtains that always parted too quickly or too slowly, finishing with: 'I can't start singing at once on the first note.'

Throughout the protest, however, he remained in pose and manner Leporello as he conceived the part—he saw Leporello as a humorous peasant-retainer, not as a gentle-man's gentleman—and later I realized that through all the pauses and interruptions of that working rehearsal Mr Evans always stayed in character. He did not put on the part like a costume: he transformed himself into the character.

The curtains were raised and lowered several times before this Leporello had them to his liking, which gave me pleasure; for nothing puts one in the mood for wonders like the dropping and lifting of vast curtains. The whisking yet majestic movement reminds the watchers that the stage itself is a personality and that the scenes which follow are, so to speak, glimpses of Jonah spending his miraculous hours inside the whale's belly. Then the curtains on their last whisk stayed uplifted and parted. The rehearsal had begun, and all ran smooth till one of the ladies hurried on, singing deliciously in a half-voice, but hampered as to movements by the yardage of her cloak and the bulk of her calash-hood.

Her distress was so obvious that the Director sprang up and, his scarf-ends horizontal behind him, raced along the gangway over the bridge, while simultaneously two men in street-clothes appeared in the wings. All three converged briskly upon the artist. She took no apparent notice of them. She was singing.

She continued to sing while the two men and the Director discussed the problem; then one man adjusted her wig, which she suffered without ceasing to sing. Others rearranged her dress, and at one moment the Director put his arm round her waist and lifted her bodily, feet clear of the ground and still singing, two yards nearer the steps. And yet, though her eyes were fixed on the conductor and her mind on her part, another side of her personality conveyed to everyone in range that it was impossible to give a performance in a cloak that pulled back from the shoulders and a hood that cramped all movement of the head, and that something must be done—done—done— and quickly too!

The odd thing was that none of these undercurrents destroyed the romantic illusion already created by the sombre, stately sets and the professional intensity of the singers. The fact that half-a-dozen strangers in modern clothes were also wandering about the vast stage merely gave the scene the inconsequence of a long, pleasing dream in which all incongruities are a matter of course. It did not seem strange that Geraint Evans was in full costume, while Siepe, the Don Giovanni, wore slacks and an orange T-shirt with his magnificent plumed hat.

The set dissolved with time into another outdoor scene, equally impressive, and dissolved again. At one period the stage became a pastoral countryside. At another we were in Don Giovanni's country house. Rows of statues wearing armour that Goliath of Gath would have found far too large for him were ranged along the walls; but the centre of interest was the group of directors in the middle of the stage. They took their time while the rightful inhabitants of Don Giovanni's banqueting-hall waited resignedly, some talking, some half-asleep, some rehearsing bits of scenes in far corners.

Then the centre of interest shifted again as Don Giovanni, standing near the footlights, suddenly threw a large bottle at Leporello, who smartly returned it. They threw the bottle at each other over and over again, as intent as tennis-players, till the central group dissolved into figures exiting briskly, and the stage woke to operatic life once more. Leporello threw back the bottle for the last time. The prima donna re-assumed her cloak, and the girl in red reappeared at the head of the bridge and nodded her satisfaction. Then for no apparent reason the curtains rushed down, closed, stayed closed, and the light in the roof went up. Break.

The drama was now transferred from the stage to the table in the stalls. Somebody brought steaming cartons of coffee on a tray, the telephone receiver was snatched from hand to hand, a procession of dim consultants materialized out of the shadows, gesticulated, shrugged and faded away again, while Italian sentences exploded against monosyllabic English responses like cars backing into lamp-posts.

At last the curtains parted again. Stage effects continued to vary. The soft singing was hypnotizing, and I was dreamily watching the setting up of the churchyard scene and admiring the vast statue of the Commendatore emerging from the dark mists of midnight, when Siepi's voice rang out with gay conviction in the remarkable statement: 'The night is clearer than day,' while clouds of rolling

midnight fog swirled about him, and instantly exposed the
weakness of the approach to opera through spectacle.

A director with a strong visual creative imagination
conceives a stage-effect and, being himself a creator, must
have it so however much it clashes with the text. Reinhardt
did exactly the same thing in his not too successful film
version of *A Midsummer Night's Dream*. He let me see a
private showing in Hollywood; but all I remember of it
today is the startling conception of Oberon. He was Erl
König, a star-lit, phosphorescent creature. He was king of
the German forests: he knew nothing of our primrose and
bluebell woodlands. His crown flashed as if it were made of
icicles. Daylight would have withered him.

> 'I with the morning's love have oft made sport;
> And, like a forester, the groves may tread,
> Even till the eastern gate, all fiery-red,
> Opening on Neptune, with fair blessed beams
> Turns into yellow gold his salt green streams.'

That is Oberon's own account of himself. But it suited
Reinhardt's genius to forget the Oberon who sat all day
playing on pipes of corn, just as it suited Zeffirelli to
ignore Don Juan's comment on the weather. A price has
to be paid for genius in a director. Fortunately one gets a
great deal back.

The rehearsal ended oddly. There was no announcement,
but suddenly the stage was empty: so was the director's
table. Mice could not have slipped away more noiselessly.
We sat on for quite a while in dead silence before realizing
that it was not another break, that everyone had gone
home. Then we stumbled out into the Market, hungry as to
the stomach, but mentally full to overflowing.

Next day was the orchestral rehearsal, and remembering
the flawless run-through of the Britton–Gielgud rehearsal,
I told my friend she need not be disappointed at missing
the first night. 'This will be exactly like one.'

It wasn't. It was like any of those familiar, dear shambles

135

which, in straight theatre, seem to be the necessary prologue to a triumph, and it made the world of opera much
more understandable.

Tuning-up began as we settled in our seats. There was a
man with a camera on a tripod. There were blue and amber
spotlights. Then the conductor arrived and began trying
over various passages, calling out incessantly to the orchestra, his whole body tense and his arm-work vigorous. Then
came the overture, uninterrupted, and the curtains opened
unchallenged, and Leporello began to pour out his extreme
discontent with the situation as melodiously as the mistle-
thrush whom, my bird-book says, 'Nature has taught to
pour forth its melody while the bleak winds of winter roar
through the leafless trees.' Then came a pause that length-
ened ominously. Surely Donna Anna and Don Giovanni
were overdue.

At that moment Donna Anna appeared at the top of the
steps. But she was alone and unravished, and trailed for-
lornly down them struggling with thin air. She was instantly followed by one of the wardrobe experts, who
hurried past her to the footlight and addressed the director's
table in a loud and injured voice.

'Giovanni isn't ready. We've been working as fast as we
possibly can, but we've got to have another three minutes.
If you'll start the overture again there is just a chance that
he'll *be* ready.'

The curtains fell!. Mozart was silenced. The conductor had
a long, private talk with the members of his orchestra.
Suddenly the man reappeared between the curtains.
'Ready now!' And this time Don Giovanni, looking extra-
ordinarily handsome, appeared at the right moment and
wrestled his Donna Anna down the steps.

The rehearsal went on, and the enjoyment of it was not
in the least impaired by the various hold-ups. At one
point the large white plumes separated themselves from
Don Giovanni's headgear and floated to the ground; but
Geraint Evans picked them up as if it were part of the

Leporello exit. The ladies' dresses hung impeccably; but Don Giovanni was still furtively doing up his collar as the Commendatore expired, and watching him I had a sudden vision of dear Philip Merivale, the actor and poet, at another dress rehearsal, just forty years ago. He was made up as Will Shakespeare and in trouble with his collar and ruff. 'It chokes me. It's all very well for George Harris to say it's correct, but I've got to be *heard*.' He was in such a frenzy that I ended by personally unhooking that collar and cutting away the frontage of the ruff. 'I shall tell George,' I said, 'that I can show him a picture of Shakespeare with at least two inches of throat showing.' 'He won't believe you,' said Philip gloomily; but George Harris, always the prop and stay of an author in trouble, very sweetly pretended to.

On the previous day one had seen the singers preparing for an orchestral rehearsal. Now the score arrived as a king comes to a public festivity, and one began to understand at last what this welcome of all the arts and crafts to a single art can mean. It was fascinating to watch the orchestra. When the curtain fell at the end of the scene and there was a wait the conductor at once began trying over various passages, talking hard in a mixture of Italian and accented English. First he sang a few bars at them, then he whistled, and always a single instrument followed his lead. Then he would point to another instrument, at the same time singing loudly: 'Yo-di, yo-di, yo-di!' and that instrument in turn would get down to it. The interval became a longish one; but it was not too long for Solti. He was still talking when a man came down from the stage to the director's table saying cryptically: 'I think he'll be all right,' and rehearsal resumed.

But not for long. Voices from the wings cried aloud and with passion: 'Not here!' Action ceased. Singers stood in a frozen fringe round the stage. Don Giovanni, central, strolled up and down adjusting his sword and cloak. At last a man came to the front of the stage and explained

at length that there was still much to do to one of the
ladies' dresses. This caused an explosion at the director's
table. 'My god, he's had an hour!' Another wait. 'Yo-di,
yo-di!' was heard once more.

Then the prima donna arrived in an impeccable costume,
and rehearsal went on. The sets succeeded each other,
dazzles of blue, silver, brown and copper. Geraint Evans
sang and acted with heart-warming charm. All through
this scene a girl in a short white coat touched up the
scenery with a large paint-brush.

Another interval; then a voice cried: 'Can you give me
eighteen?' and a spot came on. There were renewed dis-
cussions at the prompter's table. Two directors crossed the
bridge and disappeared into the wings, and another girl
came out between the curtains and addressed the orchestra
with considerable passion.

'Gentlemen, I did—I *did* make an announcement that
there will be a delay of five minutes. I'm awfully sorry.'

At which the orchestra disappeared, and a covey of
dancers flitted down into the stalls circle, easing off.

Later we had a surprise. Leporello was, as ever, imper-
turbably present and Spanish; but the Don Giovanni part
was being read by a young man in a very correct morning
suit. Presently he began to sing in a small, sweet voice
that was hardly to be heard, while simultaneously the
conductor whistled loudly. The mixture of sound was
pleasing, and the scene fascinating to watch. The Adminis-
trator wandered past us and murmured casually: 'You can't
say we're not putting on a show for you.' It then came out
that Don Giovanni had been hit on the head by a piece of
scenery and sent off to hospital.

But nobody worried. 'He'll be all right.' And of course
he was. Difficult rehearsal: impeccable show—the rule
always holds. On the first night the new production was a
triumph.

VIII

Rites of Spring

It is May 3rd, 1963, but the countryside is still winter-logged. For the last four months the wind has had its lodgings in the east with occasional excursions to the Cave of the Winds in the north, and the snow has behaved like Peter the Great when he lodged with the unfortunate John Evelyn for three bitter months.

The Autocrat of all the Russians had come over to England to acquire western culture and to learn about ship-building. Everybody agreed that this was praiseworthy, and the egalitarians are still delighted that he worked in the docks as a labourer. Evelyn had a right to be flattered when his own monarch, William III, rented Evelyn's beautiful house near Deptford so that the Czar could live near the docks. It was only for three months, King William paid all expenses, and it might have worked out very pleasantly for all concerned, if only the Czar of all the Russians had not left his western ways behind him when his day's work was over.

For Evelyn's garden was famous, and the most important thing in it was the holly-hedge—'This rare hedge, the boast of my villa.' It had taken him twenty-one years to bring it to perfection, and he harks back to the enthusiasms of the Grand Tour and his youth when he writes of it.

'Is there under heaven a more glorious object of the kind, than an impregnable hedge of about four hundred feet in length, nine feet high and five in diameter, which I can shew in my now ruined gardens at Say's Court (thanks to the Czar of Moscovy) at any time of the year, glittering with its armed and varnished leaves, the taller standards at orderly distances, blushing with their natural coral. It mocks the rudest assaults of the weather, beasts or hedge-breakers——'

But the barbarian child in the Russian ruler found it entertaining to ride in a wheelbarrow up and down the holly-hedge, and after three months it was a ruin.

Sympathy is an odd thing. I don't think I should have grown so fond of Evelyn if it hadn't been for that story and if the late disastrous spring had not done just the same to me. I, also, love a hedge, admittedly it is only fourteen feet long; but last summer it was as sleek as a black cat that has just washed itself. But the snow of 1963 has properly Peter-the-Greated it; so I find it easy to guess how Evelyn felt, at close on eighty, when he saw 'how miserably the Czar has left my house after three months making it his court.' One should never let a house furnished.

The Czar quitted the country at the end of April; but he thoughtfully left his national weather behind him, and early in May Evelyn, the passionate gardener, had to face a fresh blow—'an extraordinary great snow and frost nipping the corn and other fruits.' But 'extraordinary' was the wrong word. English weather is only extraordinary when it behaves two years running in the same way, and the countries that laugh over our preoccupation with weather don't know the half of it. It is the most important and personal problem in the lives of the English. Our literature even possesses a play with the weather for its theme.

A Play of the Weather was 'made-up' by John Heywood, who was born in the year that Cabot landed at Cape Breton and took possession of Canada on behalf of King Henry VII. Heywood was a choir-boy of the Chapel Royal, Savoy, a stone's throw from Covent Garden, and when a young man had a modest place at Court as a musician. His plays are more like character-sketches than plotted dramas, but they are very lively and very funny; for he could set down the character of the English of his day and their familiar talk as

140

easily as Chaucer or Shakespeare, and motion the reader
forward through the centuries to the country-people of
Fielding and Hardy. Also his verse, looser and freer than
later Elizabethan measures, is sometimes beautiful.

The Play of the Weather starts with a lively speech by a
personage who is discreetly called Jupiter but is understood
to be God the Father Almighty, Maker of Heaven and
Earth. Jupiter explains that there has been trouble between
Wind, Winter, Sun and Moon, again disguised as Saturn,
Phoebus, Aeolus and Phoebe. All have their grievances
against each other. Winter—

> 'Allegeth that, of long time past. . . .
> Full oft upon earth his fair frost he hath cast,
> All things hurtful to banish out of presence.
> But Phoebus, intending to keep him in silence,
> When he hath laboured all night in his powers,
> His glaring beams marreth all in two hours.'

The Sun ignores this attack, but is furious with the Moon,
who is responsible for all this unnecessary dew. Winter
backs him; then all three turn upon the Wind—

> 'For, when he is disposed his blasts to blow,
> He suffereth neither sunshine, rain nor snow.'

So God-Jupiter has descended to earth—

> 'to satisfy and content
> All manner of people which have been offended
> By any weather meet to be amended.'

On that there enters Merry Report, who is chosen as
Jupiter's go-between because of his impartiality.

> 'Cold, heat, moist, dry, hail, rain, frost, snow,
>   lightning, thunder,
> Cloudy, misty, windy, fair, foul, above head or under,
> Temperate or distemperate, whatever it be,
> I promise your lordship, all is one to me.'

141

Merry Report is the Vice of the old Morality plays, who still lingers in Punch-and-Judy shows to help Punch bang the Devil over the head. Heywood uses him as a cross between a jester, a B.B.C. interviewer and an efficient secretary who short-lists the complainants.

One of the most eloquent is a small boy—the stage directions add 'the least that can play'—who has been elected by his school-fellows to represent them.

> 'Upon agreement, with a great noise,
> "Send little Dick," cried all the boys.'

That rings true, as if little Dick were the small Heywood himself, dreaming of a white Christmas in the fields behind Covent Garden as he sings in the choir.

> 'With my godfather God I would fain have spoken,
> Desiring him to have sent me by some token
> Where I might have had great frost for my pitfalls,
> And plenty of snow to make my snowballs. . . .
> This once had, boys' lives be such as no man leads.
> O, to see my snowballs light on my fellows' heads!'

Shakespeare must have read his Heywood pretty thoroughly; for the twins of Dick are always cropping up in the plays. The little Duke of York who cheeks Richard Crookback, Mamillius, who tells ghost stories and hates being kissed by gushing ladies, the poor monkey, Macduff's son, and the small boy in *Coriolanus* who would rather see the swords and hear a drum than look upon his schoolmaster—surely these echoes of little Dick are as strong as the echoes of little Charles Dickens in David Copperfield. The small boys of England do not seem to have changed much in the last five hundred years. 'O, to see my snowballs light on my fellows' heads!'

The rest of Godfather God's petitioners are as varied as the weather of which they complain. The gentleman whose recreation is hunting wants his weather to be dry and not misty, the wind calm and still. The fine lady is afraid of getting tanned by too much sunshine. The laundress must have sunshine if the washing is to dry, and the wind-miller, the water-miller and the merchant all want different weather conditions.

Jupiter copes with superb tact, promising to each his fair proportion of storm and calm, and sends them all away contented, especially little Dick.

> 'Godfather God, I will do somewhat for you again . . .
> . . . I promise you if any snow come
> When I make my snowballs ye shall have some.'

But Merry Report, the spirit that always denies, roars with laughter.

> 'Lo, how this is brought to pass!
> Sir, now shall ye have the weather even as it was.'

Heywood and his humour is dateless.

> 'The Farmer will never be happy again,
> He carries his heart in his boots;
> For either the rain is destroying his grain
> Or the drought is destroying his roots.'

That is signed A.P.H. But A. P. Herbert is merely one of Heywood's pen-names. History is our clock, and we are all its cuckoos.

The first of May used to be London's gala. Stow says that: 'Every man on May Day in the morning would walk into the sweet meadows and green woods to rejoice their spirits with the beauty and savour of sweet flowers and with the noise of birds praising God in their kind,' and tells how Henry VIII went maying one spring and was entertained by the citizens of Blackheath dressed as Robin Hood and his men.

But the Londoner living in the Temple Bar area had no need to go that far to find the may. He had only to stroll up Fleet Street and along the Strand, dodging pot-holes and bushes, till he came across the brook to Covent

143

Garden with its grazing sheep and the remains of the monk-
ish burial-ground. Beyond it east, north and west lay the
open fields—Lincoln's Inn Fields, St Giles in the Fields,
St Martin in the Fields, the Long Acre. By the first of May,
old reckoning, hawthorn-blossom would be clothing every
bush. The May is one of England's native trinity of trees—
strength, grace, glamour: oak and ash and thorn: and to see
what thorn can be like left to itself, not clipped into hedges,
you have still only to go as far as the outlying London
commons.

The hedges were in full snow last year when I drove
to London from Sussex to attend that third of May gala at
Covent Garden. There was to be a performance of *The Rite
of Spring*, which seemed a work of supererogation with the
goddess herself performing her rites all over Sussex and
Surrey; but there was to be new choreography, new sets
and dresses, and I had been given two tickets. May has
always been my lucky month. The daily chore had to be
written, of course; but that is easy in a dawdling car.

Unfortunately whenever I looked up in the hope of
snaring an idea the South Saxon countryside was also
soodling along in the opposite direction. From down to
down the valleys were all watercolour washes of cherry and
whitebeam, the pear-trees looked like models of Milan
Cathedral, and the blurs of purple in the woods would
azure into a carpet of wild hyacinths within twenty-four
hours, and I should miss them. I should be recovering from
Spring Rites at Covent Garden. Why is one always ex-
hausted after an evening at the Ballet?

Sussex had become Surrey when I next looked up, and
the car was curving along the hilltop road running from
Hindhead past the Devil's Jumps. A gallows once stood
on the summit, and there, one September morning close on
a hundred and eighty years ago, three murderers dangled.

It is a brutal story. A young sailor—I suppose he earned
close on a pound in a month—was tramping home to
Portsmouth town, either on leave or discharged; for the

144

American war was over. Either way his pockets were full
of money and his head, one may be sure, full of dreams—
dreams of a good time coming, a wedding and a holding
of his own, pigs and chickens 'and there shall be no more
sea'. He stopped at the Red Lion Inn in Thursley, where he
found three penniless fellow sailors, Lonegan, Marshall and
Casey. They pitched him a tale, and he believed it, gave
them each a meal and promised to pay their way home as
well as his own. The four started off together; but when they
reached the Hindhead hills they stabbed the poor boy,
robbed the body and flung it into the Punchbowl.

The killers were hunted down, tried, condemned and
hanged on the top of Hindhead. But three brutes hanging
in chains—is that a fair exchange for a sweetheart and a
cottage, the changing seasons, and 'no more sea'?

The story faded into the past as we rolled down the hill
into Guildford through tunnels of the most varied and
translucent greens in the world, the beech, oak, hornbeam,
whitebeam, ash and hazel greens of an English lane.

But it was necessary to forget these green and shot-silk
effects; for a slow-moving car is a workroom in a thousand.
No domestic eruptions and interruptions are possible in a
car. There are no relations to be soothed, no intimate
friends to gossip with, no income tax papers to go through.
No irresistible invitation is sprung upon you to drop it all—
you must eat somewhere—no questionnaire on the psy-
chology of Neo-Georgian dramatists to fill in because the
letter is an artless one and recalls the vanished years. There
are no telephones. There is absolutely no need or reason to
surface for at least an hour.

Then my pencil broke and I surfaced, and was thankful,
because otherwise I should have missed a solid three-mile
stretch of dandelions on either bank. After that the dandelions recurred only in patches, but they continued with us
till we were past the grim new Guildford Cathedral, which
marks the switch from unspoiled country to the nineteen-
sixties' mixture of ancient villages and the latest London

spillovers and dormitory towns. It was a relief to reach the Robin Hood Gate and be safe once more in the peace of Richmond Park. The Park is fringed with skyscrapers; but one knows that the ample parklands cannot be encroached upon. The car-parks are discreetly placed, and the deer still roam that countryside.

It was no good trying to feed them, of course, on that glorious spring evening, although if it were winter they would have rushed the car; but young grass is better than buns. Crows and pigeons wandered among the brown, feeding creatures unnoticed. The deer did not even shy at the fluffed-out, beribboned little character which tottered along beside them intent, in its Pekinese way, on the same spring grass and spring smells.

After the Park came the commons, the river and Putney, Swinburne's Putney, the bridge and the forlorn, twisted street which deteriorates out of the King's Road and was once George III's favourite way to Kew. But the road has a charm for me because it houses a pottery which dates from the time of Charles II, and still sends clay to classes at the Central London Institute in Bolt Court, which, incidentally, adjoins Dr Johnson's house. This sounds confusing but is unavoidable; for in London the centuries are contingent, like the alleys of the Hampton Court Maze.

As we passed the World's End the last lingering regrets for the Sussex rites of spring were swallowed up by the sophisticated lure of Chelsea and its expensive antique shops. We passed a corner window which stabled an enormous merry-go-round rocking-horse, all gilt, green paint and fiery nostrils. I coveted it so much that I had to turn away and look across the barracks towards the Royal Chelsea Hospital.

The car swung left and I was home. Home smelt of the Battersea Power Station and river mists. The lawn between the long double rows of back-windows looked greener than usual; but the red may-tree had been cut down while I was away, and the inevitable bonfire had been lit, as always, directly under my bedroom windows. I thought impatiently: 'This place will never feel like home. Home is Tavistock Street, Covent Garden.' In Tavistock Street I could have had a bath and a rest, but there was not time for it in Chelsea. There was barely time for the inevitable argument about a pre-theatre meal.

'I don't *want* an egg now, dear. Have you rung for a *taxi*?'

By the time Wellington Street was reached the excitement was already wafting out of the Opera House main entrance and spreading—spreading: sometimes the happy flurry begins as far away as Leicester Square. The Market, though not directly involved, wore its most benevolent 'Enjoy yourself!' grin as the cars swung round the corner of the plant-hall and pulled up short. The Garden traffic jams have always been fantastic since the days when coaches blocked the streets because Kean was playing Shylock.

Fortunately the police plainly enjoy such occasions. The uniformed schoolboys are fatherly as they let twenty pass and stop the twenty-first, 'loving not, hating not, just choosing so,' and once off-duty they tend to linger on the steps of Bow Street Police Station to watch the Queen Mother and the great world arrive.

This is only neighbourly; for the Bow Street Police Court and the Opera House are old friends. They have had oddly similar histories: fire, riot, several rebuildings—the Police Court had two moves as well. It did not finally establish itself opposite the Opera House till the 'eighties. But already by 1856 the small force which Fielding had originated and Peel perfected had become a national institute.

So, two years later, did the rebuilt Covent Garden Theatre. In its new state it settled down to be the home of music and dance, though in name it did not become the Royal Opera House till our own day. And just as the 'Charlies', the 'Robin Red-Breasts' and the 'Peelers' (though not the 'Bobbies') have faded from the criminal memory, so have Peg Woffington, Mrs Siddons, Kemble, Kean, Mathews and Macready faded from the memory of Covent Garden audiences. The elder gods are Taglioni, Elssler, Grisi, Patti, Albani, the de Reskis, Caruso, Melba, the Russian Ballet and the de Basil Ballet. The public remembers that our own Sadler's Wells Ballet danced *The Sleeping Princess* at Covent Garden before the King and Queen and the French President and his wife in 1939; when Messel designed the decorations, the stalls blazed with jewels, and the Aurora and the Prince were Fonteyn and Helpmann. That was the best of all galas—save one.

You might say that in peacetime the auditorium of the Royal Opera House has three main aspects. There are the gay evenings, not specially distinguished, when the audience is seeing a ballet or an opera that it already knows by heart and is there purely to enjoy itself.

There are the intense evenings when a new work is being performed and everyone in the house back-seat drives.

There are the rare occasions when the theatre, the performers and the audience are consciously making history.

The mood of the evening is always indicated by the proscenium curtains. These are personalities. They hang from pelmets set directly under the frieze of gods and muses and drop some eighty feet to the stage below. They are fringed with gold tassels, and the gold wickerwork-trimming ends in oval shields at the two inner corners which carry the initials of the reigning sovereign, and these are wreathed in a gold embroidery of laurels and topped with two gold crowns studded with emeralds and rubies. The design is simple, old-fashioned, but—to use a word that suits it—elegant.

The curtains are at their most magical on run-of-the-mill evenings. We know the sort of evening it is going to be when a luminous rose-vermilion glow spreads upwards from the boards as the house-lights dim, a colour that exists, as I had always believed, in the Covent Garden

Opera House and nowhere else, till last summer I awoke one morning at sunrise and saw a woodpecker on the bird-tray outside my caravan window. He was hanging on to the edge of a mutton-bone by his claws. His body was grey with black-and-white streaks, and he had an upward-tilting beak with a vermilion topknot perched on his foolish head like a hat on an Easter Island statue. Suddenly he became aware of me, and as he tumbled upwards in a panic his rose-vermilion under-plumes were the exact colour of the Covent Garden curtains when the footlights glow.

On gay nights that glow pervades the house and warms the audience. The faces then are all vaguely familiar, the gallery is in constant telepathic communication with the stalls, and even the lazy little Hans Andersen mermaids who lean back against the circles suddenly wake up and pretend to support them.

Nobody dresses, but there are a great many defiant young beards to be seen, and the bouffant hair-do's are almost as troublesome to the rows behind as Edwardian matinée-hats used to be. Indeed if you want to know what colour is popular in any given season you have only to go to Covent Garden on a friendly night. I remember a performance of *Ondine* when the entire femininity was dressed in a moonlight range of grey, dun, brown, greeny-blue, lilac and rich black, except for three blobs of vermilion in the arena and one girl in the stalls-circle who wore pink.

But the most enjoyable nights of all occur when the house becomes one vast personage with a single enthusiasm. When the Royal Ballet had its farewell in London before its first appearance in America everybody sat on, on, on— and on—till Fonteyn and her fellow artists, who had meantime got into their street-clothes, had to come back and say goodbye all over again. I know, because I was there, to the last flurry of clapping.

On experimental nights the theatre makes a very different impression. Then, to go up the central steps and stand at the back of the auditorium is like looking in at the interior of St Paul's Cathedral from the west doors. The audience is the congregation waiting for the service to begin.

The curtains give nothing away on such nights, but hang flat and dull. Only when the house-lights darken do they assert themselves. Then, as the footlights very slowly brighten, the velvets and the golds begin to signal to the auditorium. If the red is merely intensified there will be a cheerful opening; but when the red deepens from purple to indigo, and the gold trimmings turn silver, then it is certain that the first scene will be either mysterious or pathetic.

And this is the true function of the great Covent Garden curtains. Any curtain can shut off a stage from its orchestra-pit; but these do more. They prepare the audience for the tap of the baton and the first narrative note. They say: 'Hush!' and the audience at once obeys.

During that suspended fraction of a minute it is worth turning furtively for a last look at the house. Nothing is then to be seen but a cyclorama of pinkish-grey faces backed by reddish darkness hung with aquamarines. These jewels are merely the exit lights; but they make the walls of the dome look like Aladdin's cave, and the dim circles piled upon each other add to the sense of mystery. Oblong is oblong, and triangles are triangles; but the circle is eternity. When it wears this aspect the great auditorium must be terrifying to the performers. It says: 'The ritual has begun, and revelation is expected.'

But it is always on such evenings that the stars climb highest in their sky—Ulanova as Juliet—Keschinka, once, long ago, in the centre of the de Basil Ballet Company—Tchernicheva as Francesca. Walton's *Troilus and Cressida* opened on such an evening: so did *The Trojans*, and on March 12th of the bitter so-called spring of 1963, Nureyev and Fonteyn danced for the first time in *Marguerite and Armand*. On such nights the audience realizes that its playhouse has been served for a century by genius.

Covent Garden became a dance-hall in the last war, 'for

the duration', which meant for ever. Then eternity ended, and early in 1946 the Royal Opera House Covent Garden re-opened as itself. On that evening its three aspects were united, and for once no one looked to the curtains for guidance.

For weeks all the staffs of the theatre had given their entire energy, affection, time—and coupons—to refurbish the great building, even to the little red hats of the candles, which everyone, including goodwill helpers from the Market, had sat up all night to finish. The entire theatre had been cleaned, and the Grand Foyer had been re-decorated by Messel. There were new carpets. The mar-vellous chandelier sparkled once more in the foyer, a concentration of fire and dew.

The audience was more mixed than I had ever seen it, and happy, so movingly happy. Service-dress rubbed elbows with ministerial full-dress, 1939 fashions and a few up-to-date ones from New York. There was one girl so swathed in white fox that she looked like a polar-bear. There were slacks, a sari or two, black ties, corduroys, tiaras, and the few white ties came in for a lot of admiring chaff. But any-thing and everything went that night because it was peace at last, and the crowds in the house and the crowds outside it had gathered together to relax and rejoice, laugh, shake hands and chatter like starlings.

Then the King, the Queen, Queen Mary and the Prin-cesses came in and stood in the front of the Royal Box, and one thought that the storms of clapping would shatter the wineglasses in the grand new bars. Everyone was pleased that they were using the permanent old Royal Box on the right of the circles. It meant that the occasion was not in the strict, formal sense gala. It was England's national after-war family party, and they looked at us just as much—more—than they looked at the stage. I thought to myself—our King sits there, and he and his have been us and ours since King Alfred re-made England. No other nation can say as much, or feel so proud.

151

The ballet chosen for that joyous night was *The Sleeping Beauty*. The dancers were the Ballet Company from Sadler's Wells which had become a part of our war experience. It had helped the public through the bad years and was much loved. The principal dancers were Fonteyn, Helpmann, Michael Soames, Pamela Grey, Moira Shearer, Rassine, Turner, Beryl Grey, Gordon Hamilton, Margaret Dale, Pauline Clayden, Violetta Elvin, Julia Farren, Anne Negus, Gerd Karsen, Gillian Lynne and Joan Sheldon, with a full company, as well as students from the Sadler's Wells School of Ballet. At the end, when the King at last left the Box, we were hoarse with cheering, and some of us were in tears.

And now that evening is close on twenty years ago, and though it is unforgettable most of its dancers have become as phantasmal in one's memory as the dancers of the 'thirties and 'twenties. But though the graces and the charms vanish in turn, grace and charm does not vanish from the boards of Covent Garden. It was as difficult to get in to the *Rite of Spring* gala of 1962 as it was to get in for the great reopening of 1946. Gala is always gala in Covent Garden.

Bow Street crowds and traffic were difficult on the *Rite of Spring* evening; but the police and the doorkeepers of the Opera House, the real controllers of the affair, were as calm as ever. 'Plenty of time!' they murmured as they stood on the outer steps and at the head of the great double-staircase, the staircase that demands jewels, deportment, evening-dress, and seldom gets them. But on Gala nights the staircase is a fine sight, with time to take it in. Just as the door-keepers assured us, there is always plenty of time; for everyone arrives early to watch the entry into the Royal Box.

That night the Box was in the centre of the Grand Tier with up-to-the-moment decorations which, as usual, could not quite adjust themselves to the timeless crimson and gold of the curtains. For their part these hung lifeless and impassive, like Kembles contemplating a revue. Until the lights go down it is always best to turn one's back upon the curtains on gala nights. The audience does not need them. It is merely a collection of hosts and hostesses intent on welcoming its royal guests and any other guests, say a French President or Shah of Persia, that they happened to bring with them. Perhaps that is why, on gala nights, it is the audience which provides the exciting evening, not the stage.

It is partly the fault of the programme, which is apt to provide too rich a banquet. The audience goes away as congested as if it had been present at one of Mrs Beeton's dinner-parties where, on an evening in June, the guests were liable to be served with: Clear Turtle, Salmon with Cucumber, Whitebait, Lobster cream, Fried Sweetbreads, Lamb Cutlets and Green Peas, Haunch of Venison, Farced Olives, Vol-au-vent of Strawberries, Maraschino Jelly and Iced Pudding. But Mrs Beeton was not wantonly lavish. She noted than an entrée might be taken out if so many courses were not needed.

The *Rite of Spring* Gala in 1962 was in aid of the Royal Ballet Benevolent Fund and its School Endowment Fund, and the curtains parted on a performance of *Divertissement from Napoli*. Then came Nadia Nerina and Eric Bruhn in a *pas de deux* from the *Flower Festival at Genzano*. I had never seen Bruhn dance before, and in these neo-Gothic days his classical severity and grave, easy authority made the *pas de deux*, for me, the most enjoyable ten minutes of the evening. He looked like the Charioteer set up among modern experiments in sculpture, and Nadia Nerina was a flawless partner. They were followed by Beriosova and Donald Macleary; but by that time I was sated, and angry that I could only know with my mind how good they were instead of leaning back and enjoying them.

Sylphides came after the interval, with Nureyev. His appearance was the excitement of the evening, and he could have had twenty ovations; but after the formal before-the-curtain bows he did not reappear.

Last on the programme came *The Rite of Spring*, with new choreography, dresses and sets; but it was difficult to bring a fresh mind to it so late in the evening, or to forget earlier impressions. I twice heard Stravinsky conduct the music in a concert-room—in Los Angeles of all places— and after the magical clarity of those performances the music seemed a mere bonfire blaze of sound, and there were moments when those twisting mass convolutions gave the impression that some vast raw carcass had been split open and that a dance of the intestines was going on.

It was flat going home to Chelsea in the taxi afterwards. I wanted to compare impressions with my loved ones and be hit over the head for having wrong notions, and hit back. Five years ago I should have walked down Bow Street and cut across the Plant Hall—it doesn't open till much later, but George would have let me through. There would have been a scent of newly-watered hot-house lilac in the air and the cool feel of dew. Then there would have been a little party in Tavistock Street, just one or two of us who wanted to talk over the evening. Names and opinions, likes and dislikes, fors and againsts would have shuttle-cocked across the small hours. There would have been something rather special to eat. Outside the open window Len—Len of the cheerful grin—would have been throwing down boxes to his mate.

'Daffs—daffs—good show, Miss Dane?'

'Len, it was a wonderful show.'

'That Russian chap—any good?'

'Can't wait to see him again.'

'Had a good evening, then?'

'Such a good evening!'

'That's right, Miss Dane. You enjoy yourself!'

Not any more.

IX

Twenty-two Curtains

'Thousands of daffodils, carnations, roses and freesias were thrown by the audience on to the stage at Covent Garden when Margot Fonteyn and Rudolf Nureyev danced in *Le Corsaire* on the last night of the Royal Ballet season.

'Together they took twenty-two curtain calls lasting fifteen minutes, almost twice the length of the eight-minute ballet. At the end of one of the longest ovations at Covent Garden, the audience was still showering the stage with armfuls of spring flowers.

'Nureyev gave up trying to pick them up as he clutched two enormous laurel wreaths, while Margot Fonteyn stood holding twenty bouquets.'

This is a transcript from the *Daily Telegraph* of April 4th, 1963. A friend who was present sent it to me and added his own impressions. It was true, he said, that the gallery and upper circles had showered flowers on to the stage; but it had not been the customary casual tossing of bouquets. The blossoms had been dropped separately, and being light they sank down through the vast spaces very slowly. As they floated through the beams from the arc lights they had been half transparent. It was as if clouds of luminous butterflies were fluttering about the dancers.

The evening was also the climax of the passionate affair between Covent Garden audiences and the new Russian dancer, Rudolf Nureyev. Many stars, bright-shining in their own skies, have tried to capture Garden audiences; but few have succeeded so soon and so completely.

The incomparable Siddons, for example, was anything but successful at the start. Some say that her failure was due to the intrigues of the two Drury Lane sultanas, Mrs Yates and Miss Younge; but she herself owns that Garrick's acting overthrew her as she herself later overthrew the young Macready when the intensity of her acting so shook him that he lost his words. But she was kind and prompted him, remembering, perhaps, how Garrick had once done as much for her. The jealous company had jostled her out of her place in a stage tableau; but Garrick saw what was happening, took her hand and led her down to the footlights.

But in spite of his backing the public did not like her, and after playing six or seven parts she was dismissed to the provinces once more. It was several years before her great night came and a London audience went mad about her.

Catalani was another incomparable who had to fight a hostile Covent Garden. She had twice offended. First she was a foreigner married to a man with a French name at a time when we were at war with France. Napoleon had just defeated the Austrians at Wagram, the English expedition to Walcheren had been a failure, and the public was still raw. Second, she had been engaged by the Kemble management to sing at Covent Garden during the Old Prices Riots, and the public at that moment was hating Kemble almost as much as it hated Napoleon. So the audience called her—too easy pun—'the Cat'.

> 'This is the Cat engaged to squall
> To the poor in the pigeon-holes over the boxes
> Let to the great that visit the house that Jack built.'

That insult comes from a brutal caricature of the Gillray school. It is based on 'The House that Jack Built' and is headed:

KEMBLE, hear!—John Bull advises—To save your fame—And sink your Prices!!!'

Underneath, in six sections, are rough sketches of the

rebuilt Opera House, the boxes 'let to the great', the very charming 'pigeon-holes over the boxes', Catalani pictured with the head of a cat, a Bow Street Runner (supposed to be persecuting the rioters), and finally a caricature of the Manager, the defiant John Kemble, stiffly calm and looking, in spite of the gross drawing, a little like John Gielgud taking, reluctantly, a call.

To step off the path for a moment: what a curious and interesting likeness there is between those two great players! In *The Seven Ages of Man*, when Gielgud was alone on the stage for over two hours, he constantly re-called Lawrence's portrait of John Philip Kemble, the one seated in an armchair. Kemble's head is lifted and one hand rests against his cheek in what must have been a family gesture; for that is exactly how his sister sat when Reynolds was painting her as the Tragic Muse.

Again, in Drury Lane, as the effortless Terry voice filled the huge house, stories came to mind of how the effortless Kemble voice had filled Covent Garden. By all accounts, Kemble had not the Terry fire and originality; but he had scholarship, fine taste, great power in parts that suited him, and above all the quality not often found in the actor temperament then or now—a sort of obstinate modesty. Neither he nor Gielgud have ever debauched a part. 'Speak the piece, I pray you, as I pronounced it to you.' That order has never been disobeyed by Gielgud, nor, if you trust his critics, by Kemble.

When the O. P. Riots at last ended and the hooligan public had more or less recovered its senses, Catalani was restored to favour and for nearly seven years was the only singer who counted in London. When she moved to Paris she left no rivals behind. But she did not always please the critics, and fellow professionals insisted that she was far too domineering. 'Look,' they said, 'how she behaved when she was a mere girl of fifteen in the Convent at Gubbio!'

For Angelica Catalani had been sent to school at Gubbio and of course sang in the choir. Within a few weeks the

157

place was mobbed by music-lovers, to the scandal of the devout. Authority decided that it was all the young Angelica's fault. If she would only sing a little more softly, said the Bishop—with more modesty, said the Abbess. 'Forbid all solos!' said the Bishop. 'Far better forbid her to sing at all,' said the Abbess. But Catalani could not be stopped, nor could the crowds be prevented from overwhelming the chapel and over-exciting the novices. So she was turned out of the Convent, married a fool and became the greatest singer in Europe.

She must have been worth knowing, with all her faults. She was a good woman in a spiteful world—good daughter, good wife, good mother, good friend—and admittedly immensely generous and kind. She contrived to be all these things in spite of the gift which upsets most women's sense of proportion—extreme loveliness. As to the Voice, they say that she once sang in St Paul's Cathedral accompanied by a large choir and orchestra. Out of curiosity someone climbed to the Whispering Gallery to listen, thence to the Ball, and finally into the Cross itself. At that great height the choir and the orchestra could not be heard; but the voice of Catalani rang out clear and strong, a daughter of the morning shouting for joy.

Such vitality transcends mere death. It brings her now into the room as I talk about her. There is a blackbird on the telephone-pole outside my window which every evening repeats the first five notes of a Barcarolle of the 'twenties, and the last note is always flat, which annoys Catalani. She has brilliant blue eyes and a flawless skin, and at sixty-nine she is still a beautiful creature.

I wish I had enough knowledge of music to write her life. That would be a rewarding job. I did once write a short story about her. It was called *Nightly She Sings*. She was dying when the story began, and being a good woman of course went straight to heaven. But when she got there she found that community singing was the rule, and left in a huff.

Catalani was succeeded by Jenny Lind. Jenny Lind broke her first contract to appear at Covent Garden; but London overlooked this and adored her. The great Johanna Wagner was less lucky. She was booked to appear at the Haymarket in 1850. Then Covent Garden offered her a bigger salary, and she had never read Aesop's Fable about the dog who dropped the bone in his mouth to grab the bone reflected in the water; so she deserted to Covent Garden. Law-suits followed. The end of it was that the magnificent voice was never heard in London at all. Advance publicity can be overdone.

A good many people wondered if the publicity would be too much for Nureyev; for the interest created was enough to terrify even an established public favourite. Daniel in the lions' den is always box-office, and Nureyev's is the most exciting evasion since the little Duke of Normandy escaped from Louis IV in a haycart; but at the time of his first appearance in England his own modest account of the break-away was not yet in print. So gossip, after dwelling on how very good-looking and absurdly young he was, threw in that there had never been a male dancer of such quality since the days of Nijinsky.

This startled people who had seen Nijinsky.

What is 'seeing'? What is 'hearing'? How much training must you have before you can truly see a Rembrandt or hear a Bach Chorale, or accept the huge hands of the Rima in Hyde Park as eloquent? I once watched Njinsky dance the Slave in *Scheherazade*; but I cannot claim to have seen him.

Teenagers wear prejudices like armour in their first battles with the world. My prejudice was against 'dancing'. Great pressure was put upon Edwardian young ladies to learn skirt-dancing 'like Maud Allan'. The skirts were accordion pleated. They came to the ankles. They were not kind to the figure. I suffered much in dancing-classes. When was free to go my own way all I wanted was theatre. Monday night a musical comedy, Tuesday night Shakespeare, Wednesday Shaw—and you could get into the gallery

159

for a shilling, except Covent Garden, which was half a crown. I stood in the queue all day sometimes for an opera, but never for ballet. I was fathoms five in love with words, and there are no words in ballet.

'Strange Art! that flows in silent Eloquence,
That to the pleas'd Spectator can dispence
Words without Sound, and, without speaking, Sense.

But it didn't make sense to me. I was, however, once dragged to the Diaghilieff Ballet by an enchanted fellow-student, and thanks to a good visual memory I can remember that evening in detail.

First came *Les Sylphides*. It was alluring and much more poetically lit than it was last year. It might have made a fan of me twenty years earlier if it had not been for the next ballet on the programme. This was *Scheherazade*, and *Scheherazade* frightened me to death. I had never seen anything so startling, so mad, so remote from respectable English theatre. I did not know how to think about it.

Today I realize that I shall never again see a dancer as royal as Karsavina; but at the time—that remote time—she shocked me. Today I know that Nijinsky's leap was as miraculous as the lift into the air of any creature with visible wings. But all my ignorance then saw was a man in a turban who jumped off a staircase and stood on his head to die. My companion's frenzies of delight on the way home were incomprehensible; which only shows how blind a reasonably intelligent human being can be when young and untrained, and also how impossible it is to appreciate any art-form on a single encounter.

It was not till the 'thirties that help came to me from a teak-fibred personality who, in the good years before the war, took me to the de Basil Ballet four nights a week, and on Thursdays and Sundays to the Rambert Ballet at the tiny Mercury barn. There we would sit, so happily, waiting for the curtains to part on Pearl Argyle and Hugh Laing, or Anthony Tudor's *Jardin des Lilas*. The scent of syringa filled the little barn as the dancers moved through the garden and the story, and the air grew cold with dew.

The illusion is once more strong as I write of that delicate ballet, and I hope it was beautiful as I then thought it. But Jane Austen has a biting line somewhere about 'just such a contrast with early opinion . . . as time is for ever producing between the plans and decisions of mortals, for their own instruction and their neighbours' entertainment,' and these days that cool line comes into my head sometimes and disturbs my certainties. I don't think anyone really goes to school until they are well over sixty.

At such instructive moments it is wonderfully soothing to find even that fountain of information, *The Encyclopaedia Britannica*, falling into the Jane Austen trap. I thought of that pronouncement of hers when I was looking up a date the other day in the article on Ballet.

'It seems unlikely that we shall see any revival of the best period and styles of dancing until a higher standard of grace and manners becomes fashionable in society. With the constantly increasing abolition of ceremony, courtliness of manner is bound to diminish; and only in an atmosphere of ceremony, courtesy and chivalry can the dance maintain itself in perfection.'

That pronouncement was made in 1910.

Just one—only one—little year later the Garden celebrated the coronation of King George V by a Gala night, and Karsavina and Nijinsky danced the second scene of *Le Pavilion d'Armide*. During the next fifty years London saw—as well as the Diaghilieff enchantments—Markova, Dolin, the de Basil Ballet, the Joost Ballet, and companies and stars from America, Poland, France, Spain, Scandinavia, India, Japan and Greece. The visit of the Bolshoi Ballet rounded off the second great chapter of Ballet history.

The new one, in spite of the Olympian excellence of Bruhn, must in fairness be headed 'Nureyev'.

F   161

Earlier conquerers—Ulanova, Massine, Nijinsky, Tag-lioni—had brought their armies with them. Nureyev arrived alone at the Garden. What the English Royal Ballet Company and its leading ballerina gave him by way of welcome and support is the half of a moving story: what his revolutionary imagination in turn brought to English dancing and to Fonteyn herself is the other half of the story. The last line was written in the wintry April of 1963 when, together, 'they took twenty-two curtain calls lasting fifteen minutes, almost twice the length of the eight-minute ballet.'

My first glimpse of the new star was at the *Rite of Spring* Gala, when he appeared in *Sylphides* with Chauviré; but it was a mere glimpse. That was the fault of the lighting.

Look at a bright dazzle—say car-lamps—steadily for a few minutes and your eyes invariably print flat patterns of the same shape on any object looked at afterwards. If the light has been reddish, then you see green patches. If it is white or blue the patches will be glowing red suns. In *Sylphides* the white dresses are backed by a grey-green-blue landscape, and on that particular evening the glare of the arc lamps was so strong that long before the ballet ended each figure was outlined by a complementary scarlet line, which broadened at each movement. The longer one looked the brighter the illusory scarlet flamed.

It blotted out so much of the ballet for me that I wondered if my eyes were in fault, and was relieved when a while later a critic in the *Daily Telegraph* made an identical complaint. 'The lighting puts the dancers at a distinct disadvantage. It appears that their glade is lit by acetylene flares, not by moonlight.'

So it was not easy from the fourth row of the stalls to bring away that evening any clear impression of Nureyev. The audience was well aware of young male power; but before it could settle down to enjoyment the maddening dazzle began to blur the movements of the dancers, and

162

all one knew for certain was that the newcomer made all the Sylphides look solid.

They say that when the great Adelina Patti made her triumphant debut on the same familiar Covent Garden stage the audience was so startled that it forgot to applaud because she looked about fourteen.

So, a hundred years later, did Nureyev, and again the audience was startled. Certainly he danced like a wave of the sea, but with the half contemptuous, half rebellious alarm of a schoolboy overwhelmed by too much eager femininity. The ballet might as well have been called *Hylas and the Nymphs*.

Afterwards I found myself asking: 'Where have I seen or read of someone like this before?', went to bed still puzzled, then woke up in the night suddenly, as one does, with the answer. Shelley! Translated into terms of ballet I had been watching Trelawny's account of his first glimpse of Shelley.

'I was rather put out by observing in the passage near the open door, opposite to where I sat, a pair of glittering eyes steadily fixed on mine; it was too dark to make out whom they belonged to. . . . Mrs Williams's eyes followed the direction of mine, and going to the doorway she laughingly said,

"Come in, Shelley, it's only our friend Tre, just arrived."

Swiftly gliding in . . . a tall thin stripling . . . held out both his hands. I could hardly believe as I looked at his flushed feminine face that it could be the poet. . . . He was habited like a boy, in black jacket and trousers which he seemed to have outgrown.'

But later, in *Giselle*, Nureyev's personality had altered again, much as Shelley's personality altered when he began to read aloud from the book in his hand.

'The masterly manner in which he analysed the genius of the author, his lucid interpretation of the story, and the ease with which he translated into our language the most subtle and imaginative passages of the Spanish poet, were marvellous, as was his command of the two languages. After this touch of his

163

quality I no longer doubted his identity. A dead silence ensued. Looking up, I asked

"Where is he?"

Mrs Williams said, "Who? Shelley! Oh, he comes and goes like a spirit, no one knows when or where.'"

This was exactly the effect Nureyev made when the chosen ballet gave him an opportunity to translate the story into his own idiom. This was in *Giselle* with Chauviré as his partner. It was not a gala occasion. There was no royal box and no new piece of choreography to share the audience's attention, and was clear to it well before the end of his first scene that a new poet of the dance was challenging and overthrowing all the older Albrechts.

Chauviré underlined the peasant side of Giselle. She was a sturdy plant of the open fields, not a wild-flower of the woods. When it came to the mad scene she did not droop as Fonteyn droops. Instead, harshly, she withered.

Her strong, realistic interpretation of the peasant heroine suited at that time Nureyev's interpretation of Albrecht. He played him as a boy on the edge of manhood. Now when a mature dancer plays Albrecht his remorse after the girl dies can easily seem more like fine eighteenth-century heroics than a real-life sense of guilt; but this new Albrecht was so absurdly young that it was possible to believe completely in his love-affair and yet accept his delighted welcome to his betrothed as sincere, a part of the tentative and lovely instability of youth. So swift bright things come to confusion. Again, when Albrecht-Nureyev brought his flowers and his grief to the tomb of the dead girl, the visions of his midnight were real to the audience because it was sure that they were real to him. At the end the woe of that adolescent figure crouching by the grave was so private and so cruel that it seemed an indecency to be watching it.

Coming out of the theatre afterwards into the river-chilled air of the Garden which has seen so many dancers come and go, the mood changed. One began to wonder what

would happen to a young Russian—no, Tartar—after
months of work with the English ballet—and Fonteyn.

It is difficult to believe that Fonteyn has shone in our
skies since 1935. Although at sixteen she was hailed as 'the
spirit and promise of a star', nobody today, whether the
talk is of her Ophelia, Giselle, Odette, Aurora, Chloe or
Ondine, says: 'Oh, that was the *young* Fonteyn,' or: 'She
danced that in the middle years.' She exists, and always
has, outside time, beautiful, luminous, kind, the ever-
young Ellen Terry of Ballet. But last year there arrived
suddenly out of the east a new partner for her, a dancer
technically worthy of her but of a different temperament,
race and culture and belonging to a younger generation.
What will be the effect on her, and will it be as important
as her effect on him?

A year after the partnership began it was announced
that Frederick Ashton was devising a new ballet for
Fonteyn and Nureyev. *La Dame aux Camelias* was the
story chosen.

Everybody was pleased; for if *Cinderella* is the world's
favourite fairy-tale, the love-story of Armand and Marguerite is an easy second. Dumas's novel, written just over
a hundred years ago, has fed the world of theatre ever since.
Verdi turned it into an opera. It was Bernhardt's great part.
Garbo triumphed in it. As for the later Victorian writers,
they all grew camellias. Where would that best-seller of
the 'nineties, Du Maurier's *Trilby*, have been without
them?

The general pleasure in the story underlines the fading
out of interest in tragedy. Pity and terror were too uncomfortable for nineteenth-century audiences. They preferred pathos, the pity without the purging, the tears
without the terror.

Take a beautiful woman of the half-world, let her be
sincerely in love with somebody younger than herself, let
her be persuaded to dismiss him for fear of ruining his
future, let him reproach and insult her because he does not

understand the situation. Let her develop consumption. Let him then discover the truth, return to find her dying, and break his heart over her when it is too late—there is a story that no one has ever been able to resist. But there is no terror in it: it is romantic, not tragic, and it moves its public as *The Sorrows of Werther* moved the public of Goethe's day, and as Richardson's *Clarissa* moved yet earlier sentimentalists, to tears—which is not the most wholesome of reactions. To be 'touched' by imaginary suffering is merely to enjoy a mental sexual stroking. There is titillation but no purgation. Next to the happy ending nothing is more enjoyable than the tear of sensibility.

To recognise these limitations is not to belittle the power of Dumas's story; but it is necessary to speak of them. For in 1963, just over a hundred years since the story was written, it has at last been freed from sentimentality by Fonteyn and Nureyev.

On that night their venture was preceded by a tedious rendering of a once-popular ballet. But it was no longer entertaining to watch a bald-headed old lady rolling about on the floor while beautiful young people stood by and laughed at her. The unpleasantry left one bored and unreceptive.

Yet receptiveness was needed; for the familiar curtains were behaving strangely. What is that phrase in *A Midsummer Night's Dream* about the sails of a ship growing big-bellied with the wanton wind? It exactly describes the behaviour of the curtains that evening. As the light went down they began a billowing and subsiding movement, at first gentle, then growing more and more violent till one expected them to fly out and hang horizontal like blackout curtains in a blitz. But they merely continued to heave and flatten, and when at last they drew apart and revealed the opening scene of the ballet it became clear that their unusual agitation had been a piece of intentional if not quite successful symbolism.

The Lady of the Camellias was lying on a low day-bed,

166

panting and in pain. She was turned away from the audience, and above her floated huge, cloudy images, similarly agonized, of a man's face, head and shoulders. Marguerite was dreaming of Armand, and the audience was being shown the dream. But the use of cinema-effects in combination with live theatre has never worked in the past, and I do not think it worked that night, eager as the audience was that it should. The real figure cancelled out the magic-lantern visions, and the audience wavered between two centres of interest and did not know which to watch.

But in the next scene the ballet came suddenly to life. The light, frail furnishings, the nineteenth-century costumes and group movements made an effective setting for Fonteyn. She, deliciously dressed, had all the smiling, happy charm of a young girl in love.

But she did not remain young. Sensitive artist that she is, she permitted herself to age as the story progressed, not in looks, not in beauty, but in her attitude to her lover; till, like any woman adoring a man younger than herself, she was allowing her partner to take complete charge of her personality, her movements and her emotions.

Here Nureyev's incredible swiftness of movement and his passionate alternations between boy and man had magical effects. He was the wildly flickering flame: she was the moth. She moved with him as he moved, softening him, repeating him, yet always allowing him to be in charge, till the climax came in the sofa scene. Its tenderness and beauty recalled Romeo and Juliet.

JULIET: Oh, now begone! More light and light it grows.
ROMEO: More light and light, more dark and dark our woes.

It was at this point that the audience first became aware that the two, in their perfect partnership, had forsaken pathos for tragedy and were moving to the heights.

In the stage version Marguerite has been persuaded by Armand's father that she is ruining her young lover's

167

career and has dismissed him. She then appears in public with an older, richer man. Armand gambles with her new keeper, wins and pelts her with his winnings. But in the ballet it was his laughter that overwhelmed her; it expressed such an ecstasy of hatred and contempt that the watchers gasped.

Afterwards I heard a man say disparagingly: 'But that's acting, not dancing,' and I wondered that anybody could be so ungratefully dense. Certainly we were seeing great acting; for acting, like dancing, is based on the rhythms and halts of feeling: and here we were watching dancing based on pure pain, dancing extended into universal human theatre.

Then came the almost unbearable end with Fonteyn-Marguerite alone, dying. Suddenly Nureyev-Armand came whirling, half-seen, behind the sets of the vast Covent Garden stage, the speed of his movements through space and time conveying as clearly as an actor could have done in a Marlowe speech that he had learned the truth and had been searching all Paris for his lost love. Also that he knew that in finding her he must lose her again, and for ever. The embrace of reconciliation was a dual agony.

Then in their last mimed union—'dance' is too slight a word—these two performers of genius completed the transformation of pathos into tragedy. During the woman's death-pangs the boy's arms supported her, lifting her high above him; while she, as if she no longer knew who held her, struggled vainly out of his arms in order to find him, reaching up through the empty air, blindly groping, as if it were his soul and not hers that was escaping and she was stretching out half-dead arms to clutch him back to her. Yet all was done—danced—with such grace that when later I read of the flowers falling slowly from the galleries of the great theatre on the last night of the season, I instantly saw again those two dancers in their final movements before they were lost to us behind the curtains. Then—for art has no time limits, no before or after—there

168

slid into my mind those six lines of Burns which sum up the romance of all human experience—love—death—or merely one evening at the ballet.

> 'For pleasures are like poppies spread,
> You seize the flower, the bloom is shed,
> Or like the snow-fall in the river,
> A moment white—then melts for ever. . . .
> Or like the rainbow's lovely form
> Evanishing amid the storm.'

X

Bow Street

These are a parcel of those venomous weeds
That rankly pester this fair Garden-plot.
Whose boistrous growth is such, that I must use
More policy than strength to reach their root,
And hoist them up at once.

Richard Brome.

There is always a good deal more in a garden than meets the eye on a first visit, especially if it is the garden of a house which has already weathered several centuries.

There is too much beauty to take in all at once. The surrounding woodlands, the formal terraces overlooking half a county, and the vast dewpond full of goldfish vie with the two great walled-gardens, one all scent and colour, the other full of disciplined eatables drawn up as for a review. There is the surprise, at the end of the avenue, of the peacocks' clearing with frigid peahens dipping and pecking between the stacked logs, while a couple of disregarded males transform themselves into visions of Ezekiel—'full of eyes round about'. Then comes the return past huge, casually placed trees to the cherry-tree lawn and the iris borders. It is perfection, Anglo-Saxon perfection with flashes of Jane Austen and a scent of roses by Dean Cole.

But the day comes when the rambling visitor notices an evasive little path disappearing unobtrusively between syringa boughs like the tail of a cat round the larder door, follows the trail and gets a shock. For once past the syringas the transformation is horrid. The gravel underfoot turns to cinders, and Curiosity gets its tennis-shoes blacked as it

170

walks into a garden which is the reproach of the owners who never see it and the gardeners who ill-treat it: a consciously wretched patch, one of those children of Eve whom she hid from God.

The high midden in the background is ancient, and so completely is it rounded over by fresh green nettles that it is almost beautiful. About its edges the modern rubbish-heaps cluster like huts, and are thatched with half-burned letters, tatters of circulars and worms of string. Now and again a light wind lifts the ashes and blows them through a hingeless door on to an accumulation of dead plants, bulbs untimely sprouting, broken seed-boxes and pea-sticks still rolled up in wire-netting; while the little mock-greenhouse says miserably to any Alice who will listen: 'Once I was a *real* greenhouse.'

Most ancient gardens hide such an Alsatia, and in its first two hundred years Covent Garden was no exception. The slums formed so quickly round the elegant new square that in less than twenty-five years Richard Brome, Ben Jonson's servant, was writing a play called *The Covent Garden Weeded*. In it he describes 'those venemous weeds than rankly pester this fair Garden-plot,' and derides impartially those who 'sowed so much seed of knavery and cozenage that 'tis feared would never out,' and those who attempted to do a bit of hoeing.

But for nearly a century no one took the situation seriously. Albion's head-gardeners were busy treading on each other's tails, round, round and round again in ever-lessening circles like the peacocks in the clearing getting ready for a fight, and had no time to bother about the new plantation between the City and Whitehall. They probably said to themselves that weeds always grow strongest in new-turned soil, and that it was all the fault of the actors and the artists anyway. For Covent Garden already seethed with creative intelligences, especially artists and actors: and artists are irresponsible individualists, and the theatre is the devil's church—so there you were!

Yet the heads of the stage were at least as respectable in the seventeenth and eighteenth centuries as the heads of any other business enterprise, and much more respectable than the majority of their patrons among the aristocrats of the Garden. They had put behind them the riotings of youth, married socially acceptable wives, and were part of the Establishment. Betterton, Garrick, and Davenant achieved the Abbey. It was not Theatre's fault if weeds sprang up round its stage doors.

As for the artists, most young painters are far too busy expressing themselves to be dangerous. It is true that in Victorian times it was widely believed that all artists were immoral Bohemians until they were knighted; but in earlier times the Garden was perfectly happy to have them about. They lived there by dozens, by scores, by hundreds, known and unknown, or had relatives in the Garden, or hired studios just off it, or got themselves buried in the Market churchyard: Barlow, Cleyn who taught Dobson, Hoskins who taught Cooper, Gibson the dwarf who taught Queen Anne, and his painter daughter, Freeman, Pierce who painted the ceiling of St Paul's Covent Garden, long since destroyed, Linkrink, Burman, Cheron, Closterman, Woolaston, Vandervaart, Permentier, Crosse, La Guerre, Worsedale.

All these faceless names daze the wistful amateur; but he does not pine alone. What can be more disheartening to a young modern planning his first one-man show than to be asked to study Horace Walpoles *Anecdotes of Painting*? How many of these fellow professionals has he ever heard of? How many of their paintings has he ever seen? Will his spring also be buried under—he was going to say in a well-read voice 'the snows of yester year' or if he had studied in Paris he might even say it in French; but just then his eye is caught by his morning paper, as yet unread, and he pauses appalled. For in the middle column, conspicuously headlined, it is stated that a nine-thousand-year-old city has just been unearthed in Turkey, that it is three times

172

larger than the site of Troy, and that the discoveries include *many wall-paintings of high standard*. Depression descends upon him like one of those villainous bed-testers in a murder inn. It sinks, sinks, sinks till he is squashed flat by the weight of Time and Art.

The Garden, however, is always practical. The general feelings seem to be that it is enough to remember Lely, Kneller, Hogarth, Turner, Wilson and perhaps Zoffany— because he painted Foote, the actor who played at the Lane: the picture is at the Garrick Club. Sir Joshua, of course, was not quite a Garden man, for he lived where now the Arts Theatre stands. His neighbours today are the National Portrait Gallery, the Garrick Theatre, Wyndham's Theatre and the statue of Irving—three names which cover three centuries; for, as a learned German once said to me: 'No people preserves its history *alive* as you English do.'

I think it's true. We do not put our great men's lives out of our minds because they are dead. We like to remember where they lived, and it fusses us when the house is pulled down and the site is not marked. If we preserve traditions and add to them till they become doubtful, at least it is the popular English way of preserving alive someone loved or admired or decently feared. It is impossible for the confirmed playgoer to cut down Great Newport Street without thinking of Reynolds, or cross into Cranbourn Street without remembering Wyndham or Mary Moore, or along Garrick Street without figures by the hundred pouring out down the steps of the Garrick to claim recognition and affection. By the time the Garden is reached the point of view of those possessed of second sight becomes understandable. It was once explained to Aubrey by a Scottish friend. 'There was one John du beg Mac Grigor . . . very expert in this knowledge. . . . My father . . . turned curious of this faculty, and told him he would fain learn it: to which he answered that indeed he could in three days time teach him if he pleased; but yet he would not advise him nor any man to learn it; for had he once learned, he would never be a minute of his life but he would see innumerable men and women night and day round about him . . . for which reason my father would not have it.' But once in the Garden you have it, though perhaps according to your special sympathies, whether you want it or not.

For me the painters are particularly vivid especially those of the seventeenth century. Sir Peter Lely, a foreigner, lived handsomely in a handsome house in the North Piazza. He immortalized the beauties of King Charles II's Court and gave them all swollen eyelids, hard simpers and allegorical nightdresses with one button. Kneller, another foreigner, also settled in the Piazza, also painted Court beauties, and had for his most famous sitter William III, who was half a foreigner himself; for though his mother was an English princess his father was an Oranger. Kneller makes a masterful giant on horseback of the diminutive king, and in spite of its unconscious humour it is a fine piece of painting. So it should be; for Sir Godfrey was the finest painter in the world—he said so himself. He explained that God loved all ingenious people, that painting was the most ingenious of the arts, and that he was the most ingenious of all painters. This, roughly, puts him on a level with St Luke.

His conviction of his supremacy was so strong that even his fellow artists were hypnotized into agreeing with him, and he appeared to rule long after his death, like King Solomon who stood for a year leaning on a stick before anyone dared to touch him and see if he still breathed. So Kneller stood till Reynolds's day. The young American painter, C. R. Leslie, who found Sir Joshua delightful and wrote his life delightfully, relates that one day a friend recommended the Master to use vermilion instead of lake and cadmium for his flesh tints. 'He said, looking on his hand, "I can see no vermilion in flesh."—"But did not Sir Godfrey always use vermilion?" To which he answered rather sharply, "What signified what a man used who could not colour?" ' The Kneller walking-stick was broken at last.

Kneller's house was taken over by the respected artist Sir James Thornhill, serjeant painter to Queen Anne and oddly but like Sir Christopher Wren, an M.P. He opened an academy for young artists in Kneller's forty-foot saloon, and received among his pupils a young man called William Hogarth, who shattered the peace alike of the London studios and Thornhill's home; for he went his own way, outraged conventional art, said his say—in paint—concerning contemporary manners and morals, and had the audacity to marry the sacrosanct Thornhill's daughter.

Audacity was what the world complained of most in Hogarth; though seen through Time's dispassionate glass it becomes originality married to integrity. One might call Hogarth the Fielding of painting, so closely did he match in his own art the purposes and the effects of Fielding's epics. Indeed Hogarth was a novelist and a dramatist born; but he chose to speak with paint, pencil and the graver's tools. Could he colour? *The Shrimp Girl* is answer enough.

But Hogarth once had the audacity to express himself in words. He wrote an 'I believe' and called it *The Analysis of Beauty*. The publication at once laid him wide open to the attacks of all his fellow artists as well as all the hateful Charles Churchill type of professional slander-mongers. Their jeers and their sneers buzzed about his head like wasps in a September plum-tree. Fortunately for us the book was republished in the 'fifties; for it is an invaluable yard-stick amid one's latter-day experiments in the limitless art of painting.

That extraordinary volume rams it home that what ever innovation confronted him Hogarth would have kept his mind clear of cant. He would have looked long, and might have hated what he saw and said so; but he was too great a creative artist to sneer. He had not in him the instinctive need of the intellectual eunuch to decry, any more than he

had in him the mob-need to jeer. Dogged and open-
minded he was always ready to look for vermilion in flesh
and passion in the gods. Inevitably he grew in stature till
he became one of the three rebel giants of English art.
Hogarth, Turner and Blake had each made a marriage that
was unbreakable, though each, I suppose, would have
called the wife of his spirit by a different name. Blake would
have called her Imagination, Turner—Light, Hogarth—
Humanity: and because of those unions the three artists
spent their lives in a state of opposition to all conceivable
Establishments.

Hogarth's humanity made him the chief ally of Fielding
and Coram; though it never weakened his integrity as an
artist. This is the more interesting because Dickens, who
felt the wrongs of the helpless as violently as Fielding or
Hogarth, was not always an artist when he was revolting
against social wrong. The actor in him on such occasions
easily dropped into blank verse. Hogarth never dropped
into blank paint.

Yet Dickens is a brother of that great group of ameliora-
tors, though he lived a century later. He knew his London
as tirelessly as Fielding and Hogarth knew it and as
compassionately. There are passages in his works that
cannot be read without a shudder and a horrible sense of
retrospective guilt.

'Once—it was after leaving the Abbey and turning my face
north—I came to the great steps of St Martin's church as the
clock was striking three. Suddenly, a thing that in a moment
more I should have trodden upon without seeing, rose up at
my feet with a cry of loneliness and houselessness, struck out
of it by the bell, the like of which I never heard. We then stood
face to face looking at one another, frightened by one another.
The creature was like a beetle-browed hair-lipped youth of
twenty, and it had a loose bundle of rags on, which it held
together with one of its hands. It shivered from head to foot,
and its teeth chattered, and as it stared at me—persecutor,
devil, ghost, whatever it thought me—it made with its whining

176

mouth as if it were snapping at me, like a worried dog. Intending to give this ugly object money, I put out my hand to stay it— for it recoiled as it whined and snapped— and laid my hand upon its shoulder. Instantly, it twisted out of its garment, like the young man in the New Testament, and left me standing alone with its rags in my hand.'

This encounter with an underdog—it comes from *The Uncommercial Traveller*—happened in reformed Victorian London in 1859. Imagine, then, what the life of an under-dog must have been a hundred years earlier still. But it is impossible to imagine it. One must read Fielding or look at Hogarth.

When any population is moving from one to another of Jung's 'layers of consciousness' the passage always seems to be preceded by an increase of stupid official brutality, as if a worsening of life is needed to trigger off the change. In eighteenth-century England this worsening was first publicised by a sequence of writers, artists and philanthro-pists all born within a few years of each other. Defoe was the eldest; but Gay, Swift, Hogarth and Coram were all born before the century began. The youngest of them was Henry Fielding.

In London and England the first signs that the hive was preparing to modify its habits showed up in the last years of the seventeenth century in the works of a sequence of English intellectuals and philanthropists all born within a few years of each other. Defoe was the eldest, if you exclude certain stirrings in Evelyn; but Swift and Hogarth were both born before the eighteenth century began, and so was that honorary member of the crusade, the foreigner in Maiden Lane, Voltaire. The youngest of them was Henry Fielding.

All these men knew in their different ways that cities were hells on earth for the poor and the defenceless. Defoe and Swift hammered the theme throughout their working lives. Hogarth used his art to the same end; while Coram, that best of all sea-captains, crowned the many achievements

177

of his good, practical, generous life by establishing against fierce opposition, a Hospital for the Maintenance and Education of Exposed and Deserted Children—the Foundling Hospital. One of Coram's closest friends was Hogarth, and Coram made Hogarth a Governor and Guardian of the Hospital. Hogarth's portrait of his friend still belongs to the children of the Foundation and gives them a father.

It was, oddly enough, the least violent member of the movement who brought to the subject the quickest and easiest form of needed publicity. John Gay 'whose soul sincere and free loves all mankind and flatters none' one day wrote a play with music. After it had been refused by Drury Lane the astute John Rich brought it out in the January of 1728 in Davenant's rebuilt theatre in the Fields, and it must have been one of the first pieces that Fielding, just twenty-one, saw when he settled in London. The piece, outside Shakespeare, was perhaps the most influential light play ever written in the English language. John Gay called it *The Beggar's Opera*, and the story is set in the slums of London at the turn of his century.

John Gay was no reformer for reforming's sake. He was a charming man of letters who wrote fables and light verse and had a grievance against the Court because it had offered him a job which he felt to be beneath his dignity. He was deeply loved by Pope and Swift, everywhere popular and always sheltered by his close friends, the Duchess of Queensbury and her husband. If anybody wanted to be spiteful about John Gay they would call him the nicest sort of tame cat, and like all cats he was given to independent prowlings. *Trivia: or the Art of Walking the Streets of London* was one of the results. In one of those pieces he wrote in obviously troubled imagination:

> 'Of Drury's mazy courts and dark abodes,
> The harlots' guileful paths who nightly stand
> Where Catherine Street descends into the Strand.'

for he was a sensitive creature, though his awareness of
178

misery was much like our own awareness that last year's black winter killed off bird-lives by the thousand. People of good will were sorry and put out food. What more could be done? Birds have to starve in a long black frost. It is a law of nature.

Luckily for London and humanity Gay was devoted to Swift, that man of might; for one day Swift suggested that there was a play to be made out of the mazy courts and dark abodes. Judging by his own Houyhnhnms Swift must have had in mind a play as savage as Brecht's take-over version in the nineteen-twenties; but that was not Gay's way. He used an old-fashioned cut-throat razor where his friends used daggers and Brecht a machine-gun: and his strokes of satire cut so fine that sometimes the blood did not ooze at first. But then Gay did not know misery as both Fielding and Hogarth knew it, from close contact prolonged for years, nor as Swift's raging mind nor Pope's tormented physique made them both know misery, after their fashions, from within. Gay's epitaph on himself sufficiently emphasises the basic difference in the three natures.

'Life is a Jest, and all things show it.
I thought so once, and now I know it.'

However, Gay took Swift's hint, wrote the play and called it *The Beggar's Opera*, presenting the London underworld as part of the Jest, with the gallows in the centre of the stage and the doomed, all wittily alive to the situation, dancing round it as if it were a maypole. But Gay's aim was political satire, not red revolution. Also he had his share of worldly prudence. Attack the Establishment—fine! But don't attack the audience—it's bad box-office.

Therefore Gay did not analyse the Jest so closely that people ceased to laugh. Make the public laugh, and it will pour into the theatre. Delight it's ear, and it will be kind, and there will always be a few at each performance who take his deepest meaning to their hearts, or so the dramatist hopes; for how else dare he justify to himself the success and the money. Unless the contained message is understood and handed on to succeeding generations, he and his kind have failed.

But Gay did not fail. Keats is his witness as he sits on the beach at Teignmouth writing that terrible letter to his dear Reynolds.

> ' 'twas a quiet eve,
> The rocks were silent, the wide sea did weave
> An untumultuous fringe of silver foam
> Along the flat brown sand; I was at home
> And should have been most happy—but I saw
> Too far into the sea, where every maw
> The greater on the less feeds evermore.—
> But I saw too distinct into the core
> Of an eternal fierce destruction,
> And so from happiness I far was gone.
> Still am I sick of it, and though, today,
> I've gathered young spring-leaves, and flowers gay
> Of periwinkle and wild strawberry,
> Still do I that most fierce destruction see,—
> The Shark at savage prey,—the Hawk at pounce,—
> The gentle Robin, like a Pard or Ounce,
> Ravening a Worm.'

'I saw too far into the sea—': that was the core round which, a hundred years earlier, Gay had written his *Beggar's Opera*. But it did not prevent him from providing amusing sets, pretty dresses and attractive players, and he alternates his keenest satire with spirited lyrics and 'lovely airs, fluttering round the room like doves in pairs.'

The play had hung in the balance for an act; then the audience made up its mind and rioted with delight, and has gone on delighting in the show ever since. And so it comes about that the influence of that douce gentleman, Mr John Gay, has persisted for more than two and a quarter centuries, and looks like continuing indefinitely: and all

180

because the theme is so huge, so persistent, and his treatment of it so discreet. Never outside Shakespeare has a play been written with such fantastic comprehension of what flexibility means to the interpreters of dialogue. Gay's entertainment can be presented on the stage as a fantasy, light comedy, romance or black tragedy according to the bias of the director, without in the least harming the texture of the whole.

The Beggar's Opera, after its first triumphs, had at least fifteen major revivals before Nigel Playfair put it on. He saw it in terms of Meissen china. I went sixteen times to that delicious production—which was nothing to some enthusiasts—and it ran for 1,463 performances. Towards the end of the same decade it reappeared in Germany as Brecht's *Drei-Groschen Oper*.

The later Brecht can be pretty boring and musty; but the Berlin production in 1928, when I saw it during the run, was as fresh and as startling as a violent spring storm, doing damage all over the countryside, breaking down telephone-wires, beating trees flat, flooding the roadways and striking like fork-lightning again and again, leaving fires behind it. Playfair's rose-coloured spectacles had been ground under-foot. Brecht had used Gay's plot and a lot of his dialogue, modified; but he had bypassed Gay's vision for the vision of Swift. The slums of Covent Garden had become the slums of a modern city. He had made shift with washing-line scenery and had used Kurt Weill's barrel-organ jazz. Among his lyrics was a version of Villon's *Ballad of the Hanged*.

> 'They never string us taut enough. We dangle,
> Now here, now there we sway, and look so merry:
> A knuckle bone drops like a windfall cherry,
> And over our decay the ravens wrangle.'

The play screamed its way from scene to scene, and at the end of each act the characters came down to the footlights and blasted the audience.

181

PEACHUM: Be kind? Be good? Of course we'd like to be that!
    Give to the poor? Of course! Why not, indeed?
    When we're all kind and good it's plain to see that
    God's Kingdom's come, and then we'll all be freed.
    Alas, upon this star Man goes in blindness:
    Living is scarce and men are brutes, we know it!
    Who wouldn't rather live in peace and kindness?
    But Circumstances never will allow it!

It was a play to shatter complacency. I remember going out next morning to buy a book of the words, and working out rough translations simply to satisfy the extraordinary restlessness created by some of the songs and by the acting, in particular, of Jenny the Pirate, Barbara and the Macheath. The brilliant young actress who played Jenny had the aim and style of a star knife-thrower. Years later I saw her again in a film, *The Roman Spring of Mrs Stone*. This, in turn, was one of those pieces whose influence may persist longer than anyone in the show has ever dreamed, backed as it was by Vivien Leigh's heartbreak, the Addinsell score with its death-tune sending shivers along one's spine, and the performance of the once-Jenny, humble, clean-cut and deadly as ever.

The *Drei-Groschen Oper* was later—rather comically considering all things—re-Englished and put on in London. But it was not a play for us. Our stage was still influenced by the Du Maurier school. Gielgud and Olivier were notable exceptions, but most good actors of the 'thirties reflected the mood of their masochistic decade and made a virtue of underplaying. The resentments, the aggressions of the Brecht approach were not within their range. Also the English version suffered for lack of the German Macheath—Mack the Knife—played as a vicious spiv, blood-brother to Jonathan Wilde the great. His eye glittered and he had a shark-smile for the audience as he strutted up and down chanting his barrel-organ catalogue of beastly crimes.

Nor is anyone who heard it likely to forget the final Brecht chorus. Gay had dismissed his audience with a lollipop.

182

'But think of this Maxim, and put off your Sorrow,
The Wretch of Today, may be happy Tomorrow.'

But, roughly, the German version runs like this:

'Don't be too down on vice, for vice is cold
And freezes soon enough in its own frost.
Think of the darkness and the bitter cold
That fills this shrieking valley of the lost.'

Darkness—frost—bitter cold: and we are back with Swift,
Hogarth and Fielding. They knew.

Fielding even disapproved of *The Beggar's Opera* because it encouraged society to take the situation lightly
and the underworld to preen itself on the cleverness of
its vices. Fielding couldn't accept John Gay's easy optimism.
He had worked too long in the shrieking valley of the lost.

Saintsbury once wrote that Fielding was one of the
four Atlantes of English verse and prose. 'I do not mean
that Shakespeare, Milton, Swift and Fielding are in all or
even in most respects on a level. I do not mean that the
three last are in all respects of the greatest names in
English literature. I only mean that, in a certain quality,
which for want of a better word I have chosen to call
Atlantean, they stand alone. Each of them . . . carries a
whole world on his shoulders, or looks down on a whole
world from his natural altitude. The worlds are different,
but they are worlds; and though the attitude of the giants
is different also, it agrees in all of them on the points of
competence and strength.'

Fielding's world is closer to Brecht's than to Gay's,
though Fielding himself was no hell-and-damnation revolutionary. He believed in justice; but he never willingly
tore up a tree, perhaps because he himself was a rooted
man. He could trace his line to the time of Henry II. His
grandfather was a Canon of Salisbury, his father a general
under Marlborough, his mother the daughter of a judge.
With such a varied inheritance his character was shaped
before he was born. He was schooled at Eton and Leyden

University; but he had the good fortune to be a poor man, and at twenty-one he had to depend on himself for his bread and butter. He never seems to have made much money; but in his younger days he got by on journalism and playwriting—in Bernard Shaw's opinion he might have been the leading dramatist of the century. But he ran up against the censorship, and turned to novel writing.

Fielding married for love, and the early loss of his first wife seems to have put an end to all the pleasures and follies of youth. He married again, soberly and touchingly, the maid-companion of his adored first wife. They had children and were happy; but in spite of his brilliant success as a novelist money was needed. So he secured the job of Westminster Magistrate a few weeks before the publication of *Tom Jones*, and presently settled down as Chairman of Quarter Sessions in Bow Street.

The salary was very small for the amount of work he had to do; but until Fielding's time it had been the custom for the 'trading justice' to make a good thing out of fees, perquisites and bribes. But Fielding had his own ideas. In a corrupt age he was bone-honest. In a cruel age he was possessed of the revolutionary notion that it was better to save an animal than to savage it. He was not sentimental. He was perfectly ready to send an irredeemable rogue to the gallows; but his sympathetic attitude to the wretched prostitutes, abused apprentices, starved children and three-penny thieves was a new thing come into the eighteenth century Bow Street world. He did everything he possibly could to help them, even though it meant stretching the law.

But from the beginning he recognized that alleviation was not enough. It was for men like himself to find out and remove the causes that produced crime. His great ally, Hogarth, believed that the main cause of the general misery was cheap gin—'Drunk for a penny, dead drunk for tup-pence' was an advertisement that many found impossible to resist.

Fielding agreed, but went much further. Gin—yes! But also the savage poverty and the savage laws must be got rid of, and before governments and nation would consent to such innovations crime must be reduced and the public fear of the criminals must be ended. In short, Fielding knew that he had to get control of the underworld, and for that he needed an effective police force.

The policing of London had long been a bad joke. In Elizabethan times all citizens were liable to be called upon to act as constables, much as juries are called upon today. The well-to-do generally arranged for a stand-in. As Elbow explains in *Measure for Measure*: 'I do it for some piece of money and go through withal.' Poorer folk, however, turned up in person, and how the system worked Shakespeare makes ludicrously clear in *Much Ado About Nothing*.

DOGBERRY: This is your charge: you shall comprehend all vagrom
    men; you are to bid any man stand, in the Prince's name.
SECOND WATCH: How if 'a will not stand?
DOGBERRY: Why, then, take no note of him, but let him go;
    and presently call the rest of the watch together, and thank
    God you are rid of a knave.

Considering the state of the streets it was a prudent solution; but not one that made for the public safety. On the other hand some of these watchmen were stubborn and efficient men, like a certain Constable Briggs who once defied and overcame six drunken ruffians when they stayed on after closing hours at the 'Mermaid' and then rioted through the streets. Leslie Hotson tells the story in his *Shakespeare's Sonnets Dated*, and highly entertaining it is. But on the whole the Elizabethan system worked badly, and in Charles II's time there was an attempt to organize a force of paid watchmen—'Charlies' they called them, after the King. But as the job was generally given to the old and decrepit they were of little help in guarding the streets, as Fielding points out.

'These men, armed only with a pole which some of them are scarce able to lift, are to secure the persons and houses of his majesty's subjects from the attacks from gangs of young, bold, stout, desperate and well-armed villains! If the poor old fellows should run away, no one, I think, can wonder; unless it be that they were able to make their escape.'

If anyone grudges money spent on our modern Police Force, or exclaims against the injustices of the parking regulations, let him read Fielding's *Jonathan Wilde*. Even at the end of Fielding's century Covent Garden was still a byword.

> 'Centrick in London noise and London follies,
> Proud Covent Garden blooms in smoky glory.
> For chairmen, coffee-rooms, piazzas, dollies,
> Cabbages and comedians famed in story.'

The smoky glory was a nuisance even in Evelyn's day. He inveighed bitterly against 'hellish volcanoes disgorging from brew-houses, forges, lime-kilns and other trades, one of whose funnels vomits more smoke than all the culinary and chamber fires of a whole parish.' The chairmen and the coffee-rooms have vanished; but the cabbages and comedians remain, and so does a corner of the Piazza, and the smoky glory still makes its killings in the winter.

By the 'dollies' Colman meant the women who, from its beginnings, haunted the Garden. Women without money were counted none, and the trade in young girls had been a particularly revolting one. Fielding did much to help the hundreds of helpless creatures who had been forced into the trade, especially child prostitutes like the little girl in Hogarth's *Marriage à la Mode*. Reading, in comfortable ease, of that mortal battle against the I'm-all-right-Jack-ism of the age, Fielding's stature grows till he rivals Moses overseeing the battle against the Amalekites. He stood on the hill holding the wonder-working rod of justice in his hands, and Aaron and Hur upheld him.

Gay and Hogarth were Fielding's Aaron and Hur, even though Gay's work was done before Fielding's began. The struggle was long and dreary. Only Fielding knew what his efforts cost him, and he did not say much about them. But before he died the era of the 'trading justice' had ended, and he could record that—'I had not plundered the public or the poor of those sums which men, who are always ready to plunder both as much as they can, have been pleased to suspect me of taking. On the contrary, by composing instead of inflaming the quarrels of porters and beggars . . . and by refusing to take a shilling from a man who most undoubtedly would not have another left, I had reduced an income of about five hundred pounds a year of the dirtiest money upon earth to little more than three hundred pounds; a considerable proportion of which remained with my clerk.'

Henry Fielding wrote this when he was a dying man, passing over his immense literary achievement as part of the day's work. His one vanity—he called it vanity—was that he had 'become a voluntary sacrifice to the good of the public.'

For in little over half a decade his health had been ruined by overwork, long hours and the fetid atmosphere of the court. He suffered from a combination of dropsy, asthma and gout as well as the inevitable 'intolerable fatigue'; but he was only forty-seven, and his doctor thought that he might still be restored to health, and ordered him to Bath for treatment and rest. 'But . . . while I was preparing for my journey, and when I was almost fatigued to death with several long examinations, relating to five different murders, all committed within the space of a week by different gangs of robbers—' the government summoned him to advise on the best way 'for putting an immediate end to those murders and robberies which were every day committed in the streets.'

On that he put off his cure, and in four days had sent in a fully worked-out scheme of reform. It was approved, and he was at long last given the needed money—six hundred pounds, 'at which small charge I undertook to demolish the then remaining gangs and to put the civil policy into such order that no such gangs should ever be able for the future to form themselves into bodies, or at least to remain any time formidable to the public.'

The delay added 'deep jaundice' to his state of hideous ill-health; but by August he and his small band of loyal helpers were ready for action.

'The Bow Street Runners' were so successful that Fielding was able to summarize those agonizing months between August 1753 and the end of the year in one brief statement: 'Instead of reading of murders and street robberies in the news every morning, there was in the remaining part of the month of November, not only no such thing as murder, but not even a street robbery committed. . . . In this entire freedom from street robberies during the dark months, no man will, I believe, scruple to acknowledge, that the winter of 1753 stands unrivalled during a course of many years.'

He had established law and order in London and even out of London, and laid the foundation of our modern police system. But he paid for it. His last hope of life lay in getting to a warmer climate. He said goodbye to his dearly-loved children and with his wife set out for Portugal. The details of the voyage would horrify modern travellers; but Fielding merely notes them without resentment and with the same power of seeing other people's point of view which made his novels unique. He did at last reach Lisbon, and there in a few months he died. He was forty-seven—Nelson's age at Trafalgar.

Fielding's work was taken over by his brother and assistant, John Fielding, the blind magistrate. He was in many ways very like his greater brother, upright, original and an energetic participant in the life of his day. His mounted police dealt with the plague of highwaymen: his carefully kept records made life easier for the public as well as the thief-taker. He fought against drink and gambling, and worked all his life to rescue destitute children. He may have been obstinate but he was also generous. The end of the four years' squabble between him and Garrick is character- istic of both of them. The day came when Garrick retired. Thereupon Sir John wrote him a stately letter of good wishes in the third person. Garrick, with equal stateliness, returned his compliments—also in the third person. Then, incorrigibly natural, added that Mr Garrick 'will be more cheerful if Sir John will come and dine occasionally.'

The hideous Gordon Riots broke out a little before Sir John's death: it must have seemed the ruin of his life-work. But, as always, after the showdown comes the reform, and fifty years later England was persuaded to accept an organised police force, and the 'Runners' were replaced by Sir Robert Peel's 'Bobbies'. From the beginning it was insisted that the new police were the servants and not the bullies of the public. The Police Force played up, and the public has by now grown so accustomed to ask a policeman to solve its difficulties that the reception an innocent question gets from the average New York cop can be a shock to British nerves.

For just as Florence Nightingale's influence still survives at St Thomas's, and turns a stay in a public ward of that great hospital into a holiday, so Fielding's personal attitude still influences Bow Street. Often in the 'thirties, after an evening at the Opera House, I would clear my head of the romantic fumes of *Paolo and Francesca* or *Swan Lake* by going across the road to Bow Street Police Court next day to listen to the cases, and I never sat there long without remembering Fielding.

The sitting magistrate's patient courtesy was exactly what Fielding is said to have shown, and the average officer in the witness-box went out of his way to say what good he could of the culprit, as Fielding had taught his men to do. The general feeling seemed to be that here were a lot of lame dogs to be helped over an uncomfortable stile whenever possible.

But not always. I remember one case of a man charged
with stealing a typewriter, when the politeness suddenly
became icy. The man in the dock was brash, circumstantial,
fluent. It was obvious that he was proving himself a liar
with every word that he uttered, and quite sure that he
could get away with it. Nobody liked that, and that, also,
was in the Fielding tradition. A day or two later the young
policeman who patrolled the Fruit-and-Vegetables told me
that the man was a known sneak-thief and pest.

That alert youngster was a far cry from Fielding's Bow
Street Runners or even from Peel's father-figures in old
copies of *Punch*. I used to encounter him on Sundays
patrolling the Market buildings. I knew that I was breaking
the rules by letting my dog run loose in the long empty
passages; but he turned a blind eye, mainly, I think,
because he was writing his first novel and he had to talk
to someone about it or burst. Then the war intervened,
and though I poached eggs and fried bacon for some months
at the Bow Street canteen I never saw him again nor learned
his name. I hope he survived to finish his novel and publish
it; for he knew the Garden, which is to say that he knew a
lot about distressful human nature, and was coolly tolerant
of it.

I asked him once if he had ever read Fielding. He said
no, which struck me somehow as moving; because all
unconsciously he represented Fielding's profit of all his
labour which he took under the sun. Here was young Law
and Order in a blue helmet and tunic—Fielding's vision
become a reality—and he was writing a novel.

XI

The Survivor

One of the charms of London's unique Garden has been its trick of epitomizing English history. Everything that happens in big to the whole island seems to have happened in miniature to Covent Garden. Just as the five waves of invaders—Celts, Romans, Saxons, Danes and Normans—crashed in upon Albion from the east, the north and the south, driving the earlier settlers ever farther west, so the Garden suffered its series of invasions.

The legendary Frère Pye and the sextons of St Peter's Westminster—the Abbey—were evicted by the Reformation and Henry VIII's shepherds. A century later the Earl of Bedford and his architect outed the shepherds, and Rank and Fashion moved in. But they did not stay over-long. Expensive people are always finding delicious new hide-outs for themselves and their intimates, and when enterprising outsiders hear of the new vogue and edge their way in, the first-comers are furious. 'Why can't people stay where they belong? The whole place is getting over-run. It's losing its charm. If it goes on like this we shall have to move.'

So, with the coming of the House of Hanover, Rank and Fashion moved on past rural Piccadilly to quaint Mayfair and created the West End, and the rank and file professionals—authors, actors, painters, playwrights, music-makers, journalists, wits, in all their divisions and sub-divisions—moved in to the emptying mansions and won their hundred-year struggle for living-space. They settled down in the Garden as the starlings settle every spring in the eaves of Charing Cross Station and St Martin-in-the-Fields, and create their own fashion and society.

But a century later these brain-fever birds had been edged out by the ever-expanding needs of the Market, and, where the oldest houses were so much decayed that they could not be used by the market-men, they became the dens and hide-outs of the underworld. It is only in our own day that those festering habitations were finally swept away.

But the haphazard booths and stalls of the produce-sellers were demolished, and in 1830 brick-and-stone buildings were erected on the line of the European Halle to accommodate the Market. The architect, Fowler, created a hall with a surrounding portico-walk in the centre of the Garden. It has aisles from north to south and a Central Arcade from east to west, wide enough to become a shopping-centre.

This, for a time, made the Garden once more the rage. Fashionable idlers would drive to the Market, leave their carriages to wait while they promenaded up and down the Central Avenue, visited the animal shops and fortune-tellers in the stuffy attics, observed the market-men's activities with the amused interest of visitors at a zoo, and went off at last loaded with fantastically expensive melons, grapes, peaches and pineapples. The fad did not last long; but that did not trouble the Market, which, by the middle of the nineteenth century, was supplying all London at practical prices, and London was growing like one of Wells's Boomfood children.

To follow the life, Fashion apart, of the Garden of those days one has only to read Dickens, and perhaps Thackeray though Dickens is the safer guide. Both men loved and haunted the Garden; but Thackeray wrote merely as a grown-up discovering an exciting theatre of life, while Dickens knew the Market as the countryman-born knows his fields, from the underside of the hedge. A country-bred child learns as soon as it can walk to look up, always up across the bank to the hedge above. It looks as big to a child as a row of houses to us. But because it is so huge and

192

because of the angle, its mysteries soon reveal themselves—
the spider's dark, thimble-shaped vestibule, the perfect
rounds of bird nests seen from below, and the paths of the
field-mice and the ants. I once followed an ants' M1 from one
tree to another for an eighth of a mile. It was about as broad
as the left-hand margin of a page of typescript, and as
smooth as tarmac. A country child knows, too, that where
there is chalk there may be a bee-orchis, but that it is
best not to say where, for people come and dig it up: and
it will guess that the little squirrelish chestnut burr
curled up in a nest is a dormouse. I stroked it lightly with
one finger, only once, and then I put back the leaves.

Grown-up passers-by are too tall to discover such
wonders; but if they have once known them, they will always
check as they pass; for to know that colt's-foot comes before
dandelion and the proper order of the vetches from April
to August, that is a legitimate satisfaction, like having a
natural wave or walking well. I have had a good many
godchildren in my time. I wish I could have given each
one of them that best of gifts, a country childhood.

It was from the underside of wagons and hand-carts that
Dickens observed the Garden when he was an uncared-for
small boy working in a blacking-factory in nearby Chandos
Place. When he had mismanaged his meagre allowance he
would wander supperless in the Market and stare at the
pineapples, like Meg Merrilies staring full hard against the
moon. It was those experiences which made him the most
human of our novelists, especially when he wrote of other
unhappy children, not idealized into Little Nells or Paul
Dombeys, but set down as he caught sight of them in the
Garden.

'The great waggons of cabbages, with growers' men and boys
lying asleep under them, and with sharp dogs from market-
garden neighbourhoods looking after the whole, were as good
as a party. But one of the worst night sights I know in London is
to be found in the children who prowl about the place; who sleep
in the baskets, fight for the offal, dart at any object they think

they can lay their thieving hands on, dive under the carts and barrows, dodge the constables, and are perpetually making a blunt pattering on the pavement of the Piazza with the rain of their naked feet.'

That is the heart of Dickens, throbbing.

Time, mercifully, has changed the tune. Just after the war I went to a cocktail party at Heinemann's in Great Russell Street. It was the first since 1939, and to celebrate I fished out an evening cloak, pre-war but Stiebel, and the sort of dinner-dress one never wore in the bad years. Afterwards I walked back to Tavistock Street through the bombed area between New Oxford Street and the Garden, and half-way home I came to the low wall of the water-tank—a lot of tanks had been built in the ruins of the bombed houses—and sat down to rest. A group of children were playing on the far side of the road, and when they caught sight of me the whole group scudded across the road, swift and curious as a shoal of fry. Stand still up to your naked knees in a stream in summer, and the fry will always come to nose the two inexplicable white posts.

The youngest child was not more than four. Most of them were between six and ten. They were all neatly and warmly dressed. One serious girl of eleven appeared to be in charge of the party. I couldn't imagine what they wanted, but I soon found out; for they were conversational, fearless and friendly. They wanted to examine my clothes, which appeared to fascinate them. Several small hands fingered the cloak. 'Is that real velvet? Is it pre-war?'

There was a tug at my left hand. The smallest child had seen a ring on my little finger and was gently slipping it off.

'Careful! It's very old.'

'You be careful, Alf! It's very old. A diamond, isn't it, miss? It's a diamond, Alf.'

The ring passed from hand to hand, then was fitted back on to my finger; but after that they had to handle everything I possessed. My earrings were removed by moral

194

suasion, passed round and returned. Then my brooch was taken away and examined, then a bracelet. In return they gave me information about themselves.

'Miss!'

'Yes?' But I was enjoying that 'Miss'—the last trace of eighteenth-century usage.

'Miss, Bob's been bombed. Four times! Buried up to his neck.'

'Well, I was buried three times,' said his brother, hurt.

'Not up to the neck.'

'Waist, anyway.'

'We've all been bombed except Madge.'

Madge, as one mortified, changed the subject. 'Where do you live, miss?'

'Tavistock Street. Where do you?'

It came out that they all lived on the fringe of the Garden, and that most of them were children of stage-hands at the theatres. We exchanged names and occupations, the last of my belongings was scrupulously re-pinned to my person; then as suddenly as they had come they scudded away again, quick and valiant as the tiny H.M.S. *Pickle* and her sister schooners at Trafalgar. I thought as I walked on: 'There's still hope for England.'

That was twenty years ago. The tank has long since disappeared: St Giles is unrecognisable: and the Market itself is due for yet another change of status. The word has gone forth: the latest cuckoo in the Garden must be gone by 1970.

> 'In April—come he will:
> In May—he sings all day:
> In June—he changes tune:
> In July—prepares to fly:
> In August—go he must.'

So must the Market-men go. This was being said when I first came to live in Tavistock Street nearly forty years ago; but now a date is fixed. Before 1970 the Market must evacuate itself. Maybe the Flower Halls will remain; but not, one may be sure, for long.

What will happen then? Will all the people of the Garden be lost to us? I don't believe it. When the two absurd goddesses with their Cupid and their horn of plenty no longer look towards Russell Street, when the barrow-boys have been banished and all the cats have fled, one familiar character will still be seen in the Garden six nights a week and matinées Wednesdays and Saturdays. He is the actor.

The actor was the first-comer. He has worked for the right to survive ever since those perilous days in the shady little Cockpit in Drury Lane, and it is unlikely that he will ever be forced to abdicate. Even if Theatre as we now know it ceases to exist, and he ends as he began, a busker, a joculator, he will still preserve the traditions of the Garden, which are his traditions also; for the actor, like the gipsy, does not change. His art is as old and adaptable as the humanity which it mirrors. Stage-waggon, country barn, Drury Lane or the promised New Jerusalem on the South Bank, it is all one to him. He will not die out; though he may not be aware of his own persistence nor how far he has drifted during the millennia. But gardeners know how surprisingly seedlings from the most cosseted plants will contrive to flourish, ramp indeed, in conditions remote from their first seed-bed. What is more British than the cabbage-rose? But the rose does not remember the Mendip Hills and King Arthur. It has arrived since their time. It remembers the Caucasus and Prometheus.

Another of the Garden's puzzles and delights is the freak —sport—changeling. How was it that a perfectly ordinary foxglove in my garden once produced at the top of a row of fingers a perfectly shaped canterbury-bell? I have a photograph of it, as unlikely as a mermaid. The same puzzles and delights occur in the human garden. How was an ordinary country parson able to transmit a quality which resulted in the Battle of Trafalgar? Or why should Milton bequeath to a well-read younger dramatist, not his eschatological superbity but his latent wit?

I can think of only two seventeenth-century plays of which we say: 'Love them or leave them, these are Shakespeare-size.' One was published in 1671, and the other first performed in 1700. Thirty years lies between the two plays. What possible relationship can there be between the black cypress tragedy *Samson Agonistes* and *The Way of the World*'s golden filigree.

But the relationship is easily proved. According to Evelyn the cypress 'never arrives to any perfection, but is exceedingly troublesome and chargeable to maintain—' a pretty close description of Milton's attitude to Woman. Also it is the symbol of mortality. And so—enter Delilah, the cypress-woman of English literature.

> 'But who is this? what thing of sea or land?
> Female of sex it seems,
> That so bedecked, ornate, and gay,
> Comes this way sailing
> Like a stately ship
> Of Tarsus, bound for the isles
> Of Javan or Gadire,
> With all her bravery on, and tackle trim,
> Sails filled, and streamers waving.'

But there is a certain cypress which brings neither gloom nor doom to a garden. 'It has leaves like some sorts of acacias, and these are the chief inducements for its admission into the pleasure-ground. Thus, into the pleasure-ground of Restoration comedy enters that fine lady, niece to Lady Wishfort and loves Mirabell, Congreve's Millamant, introduced to us in a sentence that acknowledges unashamed an incredible paternity.

'Here she comes, i' faith, full sail with her fan spread and her streamers out, and a shoal of fools for tenders.'

But the Delilah-Millamant progression is part of the pattern. Generation by generation the Garden men have scattered

197

the good seed. Milton hands on to Congreve, Dryden to Pope, Pepys to Boswell, Steele to Sheridan, Garrick to Kean and Olivier, Kemble to Gielgud, Fielding to Dickens, Dickens to P. G. Wodehouse; while Shaw and his flower-girl derive from the Butler who wrote *The Authoress of the Odyssey*. These are a few of the world-wide scatterings of the yearly harvests.

Meanwhile the Garden retains some of its original plants —'weeds', Mr Brome would have called them—for it is the actor, the dancer and the musician who flourish in the Garden today, and the probabilities are that they will be the plants which survive; though they came to the Garden as chancely as seeds of thistledown.

The actor grew first in Shoreditch, where the two earliest playhouses—the Curtein and the Theatre—stood near each other in what is still Curtain Road. Then he was replanted on the banks of the Thames. The Blackfriars Theatre stood on the north side, and across the river a stone's throw from the bridge stood the Hope and the Globe, Shakespeare's Globe.

But the Elizabethan City fathers squinted at the immoral theatrical enterprises of Henslowe and his fellow managers (though they approved of bear-baiting and cock-fighting), and they made things as difficult as they could. The Court, fortunately, had more liberal views. The monarch maintained a private company, and so did some of the great lords, and Society was already flitting westward. With Whitehall and the palaces of the Strand beckoning, the actor followed.

His first incursion brought him to a dubious little establishment off Drury Lane. It had once been a privately owned cockpit, and when it was transformed into a theatre it kept the name and also retained such a reputation for rowdiness that Jonson's Volpone, raging against Lady Would-be's everlasting voice and hail of words, could not say worse than: 'The Cockpit comes not near it.'

The little place became so notorious that one Shrove

198

Tuesday, about the time of Shakespeare's death, the City apprentices, who enjoyed a licensed annual frenzy of moral fervour, set fire to it. It happened that Queen Anne's servants (as the players called themselves) were actually giving a show that day; which doesn't speak well for the Cockpit's reputation, the authority of King James's consort or the 'prentices loyalty. However, the Cockpit was soon rebuilt with a punning new name—the Phoenix.

It was again damaged at the time of King Charles's execution by the Roundhead soldiery; but a third structure was in existence just before the Restoration; for the opera which Evelyn went to see in 1659 had been put on at the Phoenix in the previous year. It was Davenant's *Cruelty of the Spaniards in Peru.* But the Phoenix was pulled down a year or two later, no longer needed; for Killigrew was building a far finer house a stone's throw away.

On May 7th, 1663, the first Theatre Royal in Drury Lane was opened. It was a handsome building, the interior decorated in green and gold, and the King's company was strengthened by some of the actors from Lincoln's Inn Fields, among them Shakespeare's great-nephew, Hart, a renowned actor and the first lover of Nell Gwynne. The piece chosen for the opening was Beaumont and Fletcher's comedy *The Humorous Lieutenant.* Pepys missed the great occasion, but he went on the second day—shows opened then at three in the afternoon—and on the whole approved of the new theatre, though he thought the distance too great from the stage to the boxes 'which I am confident cannot hear'.

Also he was fussed by the way the orchestra was placed. 'The music, being below, and most of it sounding under the very stage, there is no hearing of the basses at all, nor very well of the trebles, which sure must be mended.' Later he twice complains that hail and rain came in from the roof cupola and soaked the people in the pit.

The Drury Lane theatre, off Covent Garden, has remained the unofficial National Theatre till after the last war; though the Old Vic beyond Waterloo Bridge, in its Lilian Baylis heyday, disputed the title, and so, more recently, did the Festival Hall. Today the South Bank smells April and May; for an official National Theatre has absorbed the Old Vic and is to be established not too far from the site of Shakespeare's Globe.

But the South Bank can never become a theatre-centre as the Garden is a centre of theatres. A glance at the map shows the strength of its position.

On the north lie the Kingsway and Prince's Theatres, and the Saville. Then comes the Phoenix, the Palace and the Shaftesbury Avenue theatres, and on the east of Charing Cross Road, Wyndham's and the Garrick. The Cambridge stands at the junction of Monmouth Street and Upper St Martin's Lane. The St Martin's and the Ambassadors' are in West Street. Then come the three St Martin's Lane theatres, the New, the Duke of York's and the Coliseum. Turn into the Strand and on the left is the Adelphi and the Vaudeville. The Savoy is on the right. As you turn north again the Duchess, the Strand and the Aldwych are on the left, the Theatre Royal Drury Lane faces Catherine Street and the little Fortune Theatre is on its flank. The Winter Garden, soon to be rebuilt, lies further north in Drury Lane. In Bow Street, backed up against the Market, is the Royal Opera House.

Also the Lyceum still stands between the Garden and the Strand on the site of Burleigh's palace. It was the indispensable theatre of the eighteen-eighties, Irving's theatre, Ellen Terry's theatre. As late as the nineteen-thirties we saw another Terry—John Gielgud, the last of our great Hamlets—on that memorable stage.

Irving is not forgotten. His statue stands at the foot of Charing Cross Road looking up the long, bookish thoroughfare with the National Portrait Gallery behind him, hinting at his range of characters. The pleasant open space encourages the buskers. I once saw a Houdini act there. The busker netted, roped, chained, double-chained

200

and freed himself over and over again, and the pennies showered down. The performance did not in the least impair the dignity of Sir Henry Irving, who remained benignant throughout.

But though London has given him one of its finest sites, his theatre is a dance-hall. Still, better to be a dance-hall than one of those sad old buildings wrecked by time and neglect, which have been turned into warehouses. If a theatre has to go, it is pleasant when the site is at least used as Shakespeare used his theatre, 'to please', or as the site of the Cockpit-Phoenix is used today, to comfort the London citizen.

Just over a hundred years ago an American Minister in London received a letter signed George Peabody. The writer was a rich merchant born at the end of the eighteenth century at the town now called after him—Peabody, Mass. —hard by the witch-town of Salem. George Peabody's story rivals Dick Whittington's. He began to earn his living at eleven. At twenty he was a veteran of the 1812 war. Afterwards he settled down to make an immense fortune. He was a generous-hearted man, and his benefactions to his fellow-citizens were many; but his people came from Hertfordshire, and he must have been one of those who feel the ancestral tug.

At any rate in his forties he came over to London and lived here for the rest of his life. He gave vast sums to his American neighbours, principally to help education; but he also 'attested his gratitude and attachment to the people of London' by giving a hundred and fifty thousand pounds— it became five hundred thousand before his death—'to ameliorate the condition of the poor and needy of this great metropolis and to promote their comfort and happiness.'

Comfort and happiness! George Peabody had no particular use for a baronetcy, and said so when it was offered him. The important thing to him was that the new, dirt-cheap flats should have free bathrooms, wash-houses and water-supplies. He knew how much comfort has to do with that elusive imponderable, happiness; so he gave the one and hoped that the other would follow.

His hope has not cheated him. Happiness shows itself in the way a living-place is used. The window-frames of those grim buildings are always scrubbed clean, there are few windows without boxes or at least a flowerpot, and when the Londoner gardens on his windowsill it is a sign that all is very well with him. He might not be able to tell you why the building in which he lives is called Peabody; but his flowers say thank-you for him.

The buildings themselves are austere. Sixty years ago people used to talk of them with disgust, just as we talk today of the blocks of flats between the Tate Gallery and Chelsea; but the grime of London has softened the Victorian ugliness of the Peabody buildings. They have become part of London, monuments to a great-hearted man. Also, as one of them is built on the site of the original Phoenix playhouse, George Peabody has become an honorary Covent Garden man and keeps company with the royalties, landowners, statesmen, warriors, actors and wits who have given their names to the Garden streets.

King's Street, Henrietta Street, Catherine Street and James's Street commemorate the Stuart monarchs. Burleigh Street and Exeter Street are named after Queen Elizabeth's great minister. Russell Street, Southampton Street, Tavistock Street and Bedford Street are reminders that the whole district once belonged to the Russell family. Drury Lane recalls Henry VIII's day. Parker Street gives immortality to a Mr Philip Parker who lived in the time of James I. A Mr Short had a house and garden in Short Street in the time of James II, not far from a Mr Shelton's house in Shelton Street. Mart Street and Floral Street represent the Market, and Arne Street stands for music and Dr Arne.

Bow Street is fancy; for it is said to derive the name from its shape, like the curve of a bow. As for Maiden Lane, people will tell you that a statue of the Virgin once stood at the street corner; but this derivation seems a trifle

Italianate and glib. Anyway it is a street of notables, and much history has flowed along its shabby gutters and down its passages to the Strand.

Sancroft, who was later an Archbishop of Canterbury, lived in Maiden Lane. He was the Dean of St Paul's Cathedral who was so urgent and generous over the re-building after the Great Fire. Andrew Marvel the poet lived there when he was Milton's secretary. The window of Turner's birth-room looked out on the narrow alley between Maiden Lane and the Strand, and here he exhibited his first drawings. His pencil sketch of the church with its galleries and beautiful supporting pillars still hangs in the vestry of St Paul's, Covent Garden, near the chairs ordered from a furniture-maker called Chippendale whose workshops were in St Martin's Lane.

Then there was a tavern in Maiden Lane called the Cider Club, and among those who frequented it were Thackeray, Porson, the Disraelis, father and son, and Louis Napoleon—later Napoleon III. Name upon name—it is mere chance that the little byway has not been re-christened Goldsmith Street or Wilks Street, or Voltaire Street, or Boyle Street, or the street of the Jacobites. Maiden Lane knew and harboured them all.

The Garden, rather churlishly, has ignored its artists. There is certainly an Inigo Place; but there is no Lely Lane, no Kneller's Court, no Thornhill-and-Hogarth Alley. On the other hand the actors are well seen. Betterton, Macklin, Garrick, Kemble and Kean have all had streets named after them.

The Market has not yet settled on its new home. Some people would like to see it moved to Seven Dials, if only to preserve the link with the Garden itself; for Seven Dials was once a meadow in the parish of St Giles-in-the-Fields; though it was early urbanized. In the autumn of 1694 Evelyn writes of 'the building beginning near St Giles, where seven streets make a star from a Doric pillar placed in the middle of a circular area'. At the top of the pillar there were said to be seven sundials, one for each street. The neighbourhood deteriorated with the rest of the district till it was a horrid muddle of slums. In one of the streets there were stalls where junk or damaged fruit could be bought very cheaply; but in Edwardian days it was impossible to linger more than a few minutes unless a policeman was in sight. Nobody today realizes what the old-style Bobby meant in the way of comfortable re-assurance to young women going about London alone. Seven Dials in 1963 is dingy and battle-worn but respect-able; but a heliport would be the end of the Market's Sunday morning peace. The scheme of putting it down by the Docks is much more popular. At any rate, all the porters I know are for it.

And when the Market is gone what will become of the vacated spaces? Built over? A car park? Offices? No one knows. People who love the place naturally dream dreams and see visions. Some of us want an international centre— Covent Garden always welcomed the foreigner—with Inigo's design rethought in terms of our time and its needs, always preserving the church and a central green. There might even be a clump of elms once more. Why not, when last spring the Lord Mayor planted three twenty-five foot lime-trees in Paternoster Row?

It is more likely that there will be skyscrapers, and a stream of white-collar-workers will flow away at five o'clock, exactly as the little brooks used to hurry over the fields to the Thames five hundred years ago—did I tell you that there was probably a pond once in Covent Garden? And when the offices are closed there will be no life till the rush back begins next morning; for theatre-goers will have to go along the Strand and turn up Welling-ton Street instead of cutting through the alleys and bye-ways of the old days, the pleasant days, of the Market.

There is one comfort. Time, which has levelled the Burleigh mansion and swept away the Maypole in the Strand will certainly deal just as sternly with our modernities.

Hadrian's Wall runs across England from Newcastle to the sea, and south of it the land is all green billows, undulations, hollows and mounds. There the farmers grow crops and the cattle graze. But these unevennesses were once little towns with markets and streets and dwelling-places which served the Roman defence-force. All gone now.

Give Time time enough and Time will deal with the Garden as it has dealt with the Wall, and tourists from the nearer stars will look about them with charmed incomprehension, while the Survivor entertains them with romantic, inaccurate legends of the vanished people of the Garden. He will sing them incoherent ballads, their origins too remote to be traced, about Little Tin Soldiers and Sweet Lavender, and a demi-god called Winston Caesar. Galactic archaeologists will dig in the ditch that was once Tavistock Street in the hope of uncovering the mysteries of our primitive-decadent civilisation; and will be defeated; for plastics decay and concrete crumbles. The bronze-workers left more beauty behind them than the nineteen-sixties are likely to bequeath. The last shall not be first.

Well—that is how things go in this unsatisfactory world. God give us all a good journey out of it!

They say that Paradise is a garden.

The Caravans
Midhurst
1961–63

PRINCIPAL SOURCES

Annual Register, The
ARMITAGE, GILBERT: *The History of the Bow Street Runners.*
ARUNDELL, DENNIS: *The Critic at the Opera.*
AUBREY, JOHN: *Aubrey's Brief Lives.*

BAKER, H. BARTON:
  Stories of the Streets of London.
  History of the London Stage and Its Famous Players.
BEHN, APHRA: *The Works of Aphra Behn* (Summers).
BRAYLEY, EDWARD WEDLAKE. *Londiniana.*
BRECHT, BERTOLT: *Drei-Groschen Oper.*
BROME, RICHARD: Dramatic works.
BRYANT, ARTHUR:
  Samuel Pepys, the Years of Peril.
  King Charles II.
BUTLER, SAMUEL: *Hudibras.*

CENTLIVRE, MRS: Dramatic works of.
CHANCELLOR, E. BERESFORD:
  The Annals of Covent Garden and Its Neighbourhood.
  The Annals of the Strand and Its Neighbourhood.
CIBBER, COLLEY: *An Apology for the Life of—.*
COLEMAN, JOHN: *Players and Playwrights.*
COLMAN, GEORGE: *Broad Grins.*
CONGREVE, WILLIAM: Works.
Cornhill Magazine, The.
COWARD, NOEL: *Present Laughter.*

DAVENANT, WILLIAM: Works of.
DICKENS, CHARLES: Works of.
DIPROSE, JOHN: *Some Account of the Parish of St Clement Danes.*
DISRAELI, ISAAC: *Calamities and Quarrels of Authors.*
DOBSON, AUSTIN: *A Paladin of Philanthropy.*
DODSLEY, ROBERT: *Old English Plays.*
DRYDEN, JOHN:
  Essays of Dryden (Ker).
  Works

Encyclopaedia Britannica.

Evans Music and Supper Rooms: Pamphlets and Programmes *circa* 1859.

EVELYN, JOHN:
  The Diaries of John Evelyn (Dobson).
  Silva (Hunter).

FERRIS, GEORGE T.: *Great Singers.*
FIELDING, HENRY: Collected works.
FITZGERALD, PERCY: *Chronicles of Bow Street Police Office.*
FLOWER, NEWMAN: *George Frideric Handel.*
FORSTER, JOHN: *The Life of Charles Dickens.*
FRENCH, YVONNE: *Mrs Siddons: Tragic Actress.*

GAY, JOHN: Works.
GAYE, PHOEBE FENWICK: *John Gay.*
GAYLEY, CHARLES MILLS: *Representative English Comedies.*
GIELGUD, JOHN: *Early Stages.*
GILLILAND, THOMAS: *The Dramatic Mirror.*
GOLDSMITH, OLIVER: Works.
GOSSE, EDMUND: *Life of William Congreve.*
GRAY, W. FORBES: *The Poets Laureates of England.*

HARE, AUGUSTUS J. C.: *Walks in London.*
Harleian Miscellany, The.
HASKELL, ARNOLD: *Diaghilieff.*
HAYDON, BENJAMIN ROBERT: *The Autobiography and Journals of Benjamin Robert Haydon* (Elwin).
HOBHOUSE, CHRISTOPHER: *Fox.*
HOGARTH, WILLIAM: *The Analysis of Beauty.*
HOTSON, LESLIE: *Shakespeare's Sonnets Dated.*
HUGHES, M. V.: *London at Home.*
HUGHES, SPIKE: *Great Opera Houses.*
HUNT, LEIGH: *Correspondence of Leigh Hunt.* Edited by his son.

Illustrated London News, The.

JACOBS, REGINALD: *Covent Garden, its Romance and History.*
JESSE, JOHN HENEAGE:
  London and its Celebrities.
  Literary and Historical Memorials of London.

208

JOHNSON, SAMUEL: *Lives of the English Poets.*
JONSON, BEN:
   The Works of Ben Jonson (Gifford).
   The Works of Ben Jonson (Mermaid Series).

KEATS, JOHN: Works.
KEMBLE, FANNY: *Diaries of Fanny Kemble.*
KNIGHT, CHARLES: *London.*
KNIGHT, L. C.: *Drama and Society in the Age of Jonson.*
KNIGHT, G. WILSON: *The Golden Labyrinth.*

LAMB, CHARLES:
   Essays of Elia,
   The Letters of Charles Lamb (Ainger).
LESLIE, CHARLES ROBERT:
   Life and Times of Joshua Reynolds.
   Autobiographical Recollections.
LOCKHART, J. G.: *Memoirs of the Life of Sir Walter Scott.*
London Stage, The.
LOWE, ROBERT W.: *Thomas Betterton.*
LUCAS, E. V.: *The Second Post.*

MACAULAY, LORD: *History of England.*
MACHYN, HENRY: *Diary of Henry Machyn*, 1556-1563.
MACMICHAEL, J. HOLDEN: *The Story of Charing Cross and Its Immediate Neighbourhood.*
MACREADY: *Macready's Diaries.*
MARTELLI, GEORGE: *Jemmy Twitcher: A Life of John Montague, Fourth Earl of Sandwich.*
MAYHEW, HENRY: *London Labour and the London Poor.*
McKECHINIE, SAMUEL: *Popular Entertainment through the Ages.*
MILTON, JOHN: *Samson Agonistes.*
MITTEN: *Maps of Old London.*

NICOLL, ALLARDYCE:
   The English Theatre.
   Dryden as an Adapter of Shakespeare.

OMAN, CAROLA: *David Garrick.*
Oxford Book of Eighteenth Century Verse, The.
Oxford English Dictionary, The.

PARKER, JOHN: *Who's Who In the Theatre.*
PASCO, CHARLES EYRE: *The Joyous Neighbourhood of Covent Garden—a literary Souvenir of the Tavistock Hotel.*
PEPYS, SAMUEL: *The Diary of Samuel Pepys* (Wheatley).
PINDAR, PETER: *The Volunteer Laureate.*
PINTO, VIVIAN DE SOLA: *Enthusiast in Wit* (re Rochester).
POPE, ALEXANDER: Works.
PRINGLE, PATRICK: *Hue and Cry.*

QUENNELL, PETER: *Hogarth's Progress.*

ROCHESTER, EARL OF: *Lyrics and Satires of John Wilmot, Second Earl of Rochester.*
ROSENTHAL, HAROLD: *Two Centuries of Opera at Covent Garden.*
ROYDE-SMITH, NAOMI: *The Private Life of Mrs Siddons.*
RUSSELL, W. CLARK: *Representative Actors.*

SCOTT, WALTER: *Life of John Dryden.*
SHAKESPEARE: *A New Variorum Edition of Shakespeare* (Furness).
SMITH, CHARLES MANLY: *Curiosities of London Life.*
SPENCE, JOSEPH: *Anecdotes, Observations and Characters of Books and Men.*
STEELE, RICHARD and ADDISON, JOSEPH:
  The Spectator.
  The Tatler.
STEELE, RICHARD: *Periodical Journalism* 1714-16.
STOW: *A Survey of the Cities of London and Westminster.*
STRYPE: *Strype's Continuation of Stow.*

TIMBS, JOHN:
  The Romance of London.
  Walks and Talks About London.
  History of Clubs and Club Life.
  Nooks and Corners of English Life, etc.

TRELAWNEY, EDWARD JOHN: *Recollections of Shelley and Byron.*
TREWIN, J. C.: *Mr Macready.*

VOLTAIRE, FRANÇOIS M. A. DE:
  Letters Concerning the English Nation.
  The Princess of Babylon.

WALPOLE, HORACE:
  Anecdotes of Painting in England.
  The Letters of Horace Walpole.
WHEATLEY, HENRY B.: *London Past and Present.*
WRIGHT, ERIC WALTER: *The Rise of English Opera.*